In the Name of Allah,
the Compassionate, the Merciful,
Praise be to Allah, Lord of the Universe,
and Peace and Prayers be upon
His Final Prophet and Messenger.

"... and say: My Lord!
Cause Me to Grow in Knowledge."

ACKNOWLEDGEMENT

The joint sponsorship by the Inter-Religious Peace Colloquium: The Muslim-Jewish-Christian Conference of the "Trialogue of the Abrahamic Faiths" meetings held at the American Academy of Religion annual conference in New York in 1979, and their generous assistance in the publication of the first edition of this book are gratefully acknowledged.

TRIALOGUE OF THE
ABRAHAMIC FAITHS

First Edition
(1402/1982)

Second Edition
(1406/1986)

Third Edition
(1411/1991)

Fourth Edition
(1415/1995)

TRIALOGUE
OF THE
ABRAHAMIC FAITHS

Papers presented to the
Islamic Studies Group of
American Academy of Religion

Edited by
Ismā'īl Rājī al Fārūqī

amana publications
Beltsville, Maryland USA

Issues in Islamic Thought No. (1)

©Copyright 1411 AH / 1991 AC by

The International Institute of Islamic Thought
555 Grove Street
Herndon, Virginia 22070-4705 U.S.A.

Library of Congress Cataloging-in-Publication Data

Trialogue of the Abrahamic faiths : papers presented to the Islamic
    Studies Group of American Academy of Religion / edited by
    Ismā'īl Rājī al Fārūqī. -- 4th ed.
        p. 120 cm. 22 1/2 x 15 -- (Issues of Islamic thought ; no. 1)
    Originally published: 1st ed. Herndon, Va. : International
    Institute of Islamic Thought, 1982.
    Includes bibliographical references and index.
    ISBN 0-915957-25-6
    1. Islam--Relations--Judaism--Congresses. 2. Judaism--
Relations--Islam--Congresses. 3. Islam--Relations--Christianity--
Congresses.
4. Chrisitianity and other religions--Islam--Congresses.
5. Christianity and other religions--Judaism--Congresses.
6. Judaism--Relations--Christianity--Congresses. I. Al Fārūqī,
Ismā'īl R., 1921- II. American Academy of Religion. Islamic
Studies Group. III. Series.
[BP172. T75   1995]
291.1'72--dc20   95-5120
                                                        CIP

Printed in the United States of America by International Graphics Printing Service
10710 Tucker Street, Beltsville, Maryland 20705, U.S.A. Tel. (301) 595-5999 Fax: (301) 595-5888

CONTENTS

INTRODUCTION TO THE THIRD EDITION

As the birthplace of the three Abrahamic faiths, Judaism, Christianity, and Islam, the Middle East has an importance for modern man that goes far beyond the obvious. If the war in the Gulf highlighted the strategic and economic elements of that importance, it also left the world with the clear understanding that in order to achieve a lasting peace the members of the three Abrahamic faith communities will have to learn to come to terms with one another.

The beginning of any such process must be at the level of faith itself, as faith is the common ground of understanding from which all ethics and values are drawn. It is for this reason, then, that the International Institute of Islamic Thought is pleased to present a new edition of the *Trialogue of the Abrahamic Faiths*. Certainly, it is clear from their papers that the contributors to this volume shared the view that an increased understanding of each of these three faiths would lead to an increase in mutual respect and tolerance; and certainly, it is with this hope in mind that the reader should approach this unique and challenging work.

For the ease of the reader a number of indices have been added to this edition. These include a complete index of Biblical and Qur'anic verses, as well as general and subject index. Care has been taken to ensure the correctness and authenticity of the text.

The International Institute of Islamic Thought welcomes its readers to the third edition of the *Trialogue*, and urges them to open their hearts and their minds to all of their brothers and sisters in faith.

Dr. Ṭāhā Jābir al 'Alwānī
President, International
Institute of Islamic Thought
Ramadan, 1411 / April, 1991

FOREWORD

For its 1979 convention held in New York City, the American Academy of Religion (AAR) organized a very unusual meeting. Its Islāmic Studies Committee entertained the vision of bringing together members of the Jewish, Christian and Muslim academic communities in the United States to dialogue with one another on the subject of their own faiths. This was a novel undertaking unprecedented in AAR history, the Islāmic Studies Committee sought and obtained the assistance of the Inter-Religious Peace Colloquium (later called The Muslim-Jewish-Christian Conference – MJCC), the only western body with any experience in the matter.

In the early Middle Ages, the caliphal courts of Damascus, Baghdad and Cordova witnessed countless meetings of Jews, Christians and Muslims in which the learned adherents debated the three faiths. The reigning culture gave such honor to the three religions and such respect to their principals and institutions that inter-religious debate was the subject of *salon* conversation, a public pastime. Their deliberations gave birth to the discipline of comparative religion *('Ilm al Milal wa al Niḥal)* which left us a great legacy. Hardly any of the great scholars who lived in or near these great cities did not find the interest or time to contribute significantly to that legacy of human learning. Since those days, unfortunately, no such encounters have taken place; and the discipline has been dormant until the present century. The works of al Ash'arī, Ibn Ḥazm, al Baghdādī, al Nawbakhtī, al Shahristānī, al Bīrūnī, some of the luminaries of the discipline, are studied around the world; but these constitute only the exposed tip of any iceberg of literature on the subject.

In our days, the MJCC was the only attempt made by this generation to bring together Jewish, Christian and Muslim scholars to communicate with one another on matters of religion. Its purpose was rapprochement and mutual understanding between the three Abrahamic faiths. Organized in 1974 through the tireless and noble effort of Msgr. Dr. Joseph Gremillion, former Director of the Vatican's Justice and Peace Commission, and his colleagues, the MJCC held two international conferences – one in Bellagio Italy) in 1975 and another in Lisbon (Portugal) in 1977. The former dealt with "Food/Energy and the Major Faiths," the latter, with "World Faiths and the New World Order." The MJCC published the proceedings of the two meetings in books carrying these themes as titles.

The MJCC meetings were the first to be held in modern times. They were genuinely ecumenical in that they were attended by people of vision who looked forward to inter-religious understanding and cooperation as the only alternative to the hostility which has dominated relations between the three faith communities. They were convinced that ignorance and misunderstanding, the twin feeders of inter-religious hostility, ought to be cut off a serious return to dialogue. But no dialogue between the three Abrahamic faiths was in evidence anywhere in the world.

Jewish-Christian dialogue has been making great strides since the end of World War II. It has already established for itself a viable tradition and a rich literature. Christian-Muslim dialogue, on the other hand, is to this day still in its infancy, struggling desperately to survive. For the most part, it has been a Christian initiative, reluctantly entered into by either side. It still has nothing, or nearly nothing, to show for itself. The Christians who enter it do so with a conscience split between the guilts of colonialism and mission, and loyalty to their countries' continuing ascendency in world power. The Muslims, for their part, were always the invited guests of the Christians, and felt it. Neither did any other Muslims elect them to participate, nor did they appoint themselves to do so. Rather, they were selected by the Church authorities in expectation of collaboration with their hosts.

On one occasion only did the Muslims take the initiative and play host to the dialogue: at the Tripoli (Libya) conference (1974) between the Vatican and some oriental Christian churches, and Muslims from around the world. The Protestant churches, the World Council of Churches, and the Greek and Russian Orthodox Churches merely sent observers. This meeting too failed. Although the Muslims sought and obtained agreement on a number of issues affecting the two communities. The Christian delegation repudiated the agreement at the airport, minutes before its departure, to the consternation of all conference participants. Neither Muslims nor Christians pursued the matter, or followed up the resolutions with programs for their actualization.

The malaise was one and the same: No dialogue can succeed where one party is "host" and the others are "invited guests." Every party must be host and feel itself so. Every party must feel absolutely free to speak its own mind, free of both burdens at once: that of obligation to the other party, as well as that of loyalty to one's organization or government. There can be no "upper hand" and "lower hand" in dialogue; all "hands" must be equal. Moreover, candid respect of the other faiths by each party is equally a necessity. The Christian-Muslim dialogue has failed precisely because these prerequisites were absent. Last but not least, Muslim-Jewish dialogue is still non-existent. It has absolutely nothing to show for itself; no precedent, not even a hypothetical agenda. The creation of the state of Israel and the continuous hostility this has engendered between Jewry and the Muslim World prevented any religious dialogue from taking place.

The barrenness of this history in modern times puts the achievement of the MJCC in a very special light, a light which becomes all the brighter when we consider the world's dire need for mutual understanding between the three faiths. All the more pity therefore that the MJCC could not muster the public support necessary to survive. Its last public activity was to sponsor the "Trialogue of the Abrahamic Faiths" organized by the AAR Islāmic Studies Group. The meetings were held under their joint sponsorship. The late, Cardinal Sergio Pignedoli, President of the Secretariat for Non-Christians, the Vatican, was invited to deliver the keynote address of the Trialogue.

Nine prominent scholars were chosen from the American academic community (three Jews, three Christians, and three Muslims) to present statements on assigned topics. The three topics agreed upon were: "The Other Faiths," "The Nation-State as Form of Social Organization" and "The Faith-Community as Trans-national Actor for Justice and Peace." This book is a record of the statements read at the meetings, and reworked by their authors thereafter.

This is a first step toward dialogue between the three faiths, a step which requires information about and understanding of the perspectives of the faiths concerned. We believe that the very juxtaposition of the three statements on each of the three topics in one publication is an "act" of comparative religion certain to open avenues for future thought and discussion. And we hope that this publication will be followed by many others which scholars of the three faiths will prepare in dialogue and cooperation with one another.

Ismā'īl R. al Fārūqī
Chairman
Islamic Studies Group
American Academy of Religion

KEYNOTE ADDRESS

The Catholic Church and the Jewish and Muslim faiths: trialogue of the three Abrahamic faiths

The late *Cardinal Sergio Pignedoli*
The Vatican

"You shall be the father of a host of nations" (Gen. 17:4)

It is an honour for me to have been asked to give this address by the American Academy of Religion. I am happy to give it, not only because the invitation comes from sincere "friends of God", but also because I am convinced that the theme on which I have been invited to speak corresponds to a deeply felt need in the world of today: namely, the question of the presence of God and of religious values in the history of individuals and entire peoples.

The faith of Abraham, who is rightly considered by our three religions as "the father of our faith", will be the subject of my reflections. I shall remain within the limits of its essential values and not enter into a consideration of the differences of these religions, united as they are in their acceptance of Abrahamic faith and in their considering it to be a source of inspiration and a guide for human life, capable of giving a satisfactory response to the essential problems of man.

I think it is superfluous for me to say that since our purpose is to consider in its substance this faith which so happily unites us, there is no need for me to go back over past history with its tale of mutual misunderstandings, injustices, faults, lack of generosity and so on. It would have no point, since the purpose of our meeting is that it should be one of friendship. Certainly we must study the past and learn from it, but life must above all look to the present and to the future. The Christian mystic Meister Eckhart said: "If a man has turned away from sin and left it behind him, then the good God looks on that man as if he had never sinned ... If He finds him well disposed, God does not consider what he has been: God is a God of the present; as He finds you, so He takes you and accepts you. He does not ask what you have been, but what you are now".

1. Our faith in God

The faith we have inherited from Abraham has as its central pivot a monotheism free from uncertainties or equivocations: we profess one God, a God who is personal, the Creator of the world, provident, active in history but separated from it by an infinite gulf, the judge of men's actions, and who has spoken to men through the prophets. The Sacred Books and the traditions of our three religions admit no shadow of doubt on this fundamental point. This basic unity of faith is of such importance that it allows us to consider our differences with serenity and with a sense of perspective: it does not mean that we minimize these differences and still less that we renounce the points that separate us. But it does mean that we can speak together in an atmosphere of understanding and friendship, because we are all "believers in the same God"!

Without rejecting the word "dialogue", so rich in meaning and in the spirit of brotherhood, I would prefer to use the word "encounter" since it seems to express more vividly the fact that all of us, as individuals and as communities (Jews, Christians and Muslims), are vitally "committed" to giving absolute priority of respect, submission and love to the One God who accompanies us with His providence and who, at the end of time, will judge us "according to the Law of right and wrong which He has written in our heart" (Newman).

Throughout the centuries our three religions of prophetic monotheism have remained unswerving in adherence to their faith, in spite of the dissensions and differences regarding points to which we will refer later. It is sufficient here to recall explicit expressions as given in key texts: "Hear, O Israel, the Lord is our God, one Lord, and you must love the Lord your God with all your heart and soul and strength. These commandments which I give you this day are to be kept in your heart; you shall repeat them to your sons, and speak of them indoors and out of doors, when you lie down and when you rise. Bind them as a sign on the hand and wear them as a phylactery on the forehead; write them up on the doorposts of your houses and your gates" (Deut. 6: 4-9).

Even the Romans, jealous of the imperial authority that they regarded as invested with divine power, had to accept Jewish insistence that to God alone was reserved a name "which had no equal". This name was above any sovereignty, including that of Caesar, and the Roman insignia with the Capitoline gods were not allowed into the holy city of Jerusalem. Every attempt to flout this norm was vigorously resisted; no persecution succeeded in breaking it.

The identical phenomenon was found in Christianity: its fidelity to the One God, with the exclusion of any other divinity, was the fact that revealed to the Roman authorities the true nature of Christianity and its irreconcilability with paganism.

As regards the faith of Islām, we have only to read again that wonderful list of the ninety-nine beautiful names of God (*Asmā' Allāh al ḥusnā*) to be forcibly aware of the unshakeable and jealously guarded Muslim faith in the One God of Abraham.

If what C.S. Lewis asserts is true, namely that "the geography of the spiritual world is different from that of the physical world: in the physical world contact between countries is at the frontiers, in the spiritual world contact is at the centre", then we can say that the Jewish-Christian-Muslim world make contact and meet at the very heart of a common faith. This religious affinity has always met with difficulties and it would be dishonest not to acknowledge this. However, there have always been through the centuries, thanks to the merciful God to whom we lift up our hearts, examples of mutual understanding and even collaboration.

We can think, for example, in the high Middle Ages of the Toledo conversations and of those at Cordoba, where, in the very palace of the Archbishop, Christians, Muslims and Jews met together in discussion. We could think too of the writings of Maimonides, Ibn Rushd and al Fārābī, and of St. Thomas, writings that influenced one another and contributed not a little to the forming of medieval civilization.

For a time during the Middle Ages, Arabic was the language most commonly used among Jewish writers. A significant example is "The Introduction to the Duties of the Heart" by Bahya ibn Paquda; it was written in Arabic, translated into Hebrew, and, a later time, was also to come to the attention of Christians. It is in this work that we find a quotation, evidently taken from the Gospel of Matthew, 5: 33-37, and with reference to Jesus: "A wise man said to his disciples: the Law permits us to swear the truth in the name of the Lord, but I say to you never swear either for the truth or for falsehood. Let what you say be simply 'yes' or 'no'". Raymond Lull understood in depth the common platform of the three religions and the good that could derive from it: we see this in "The Book of the Pagan and the Three Wise Men" (1277). Nicholas of Cusa in his work "De pace fidei" wrote of the harmony of the three great religions and of its possible influence for the peace of the world. It should be noted that he wrote this work immediately after the fall of Constantinople, a time when others were thinking of launching a crusade to recapture it!

It is probably true that these "happy instances" were not typical but rather singular and isolated events, while over many years and even centuries there were reciprocal misunderstandings and suspicions, conflicts and persecutions, in which it is difficult, or better, impossible to determine the responsibilities of the different sides. It is my sincere and humble opinion that the best road to follow is that of sharing sorrow for what has happened in the past and of choosing resolutely, all

3

of us, to open ourselves not only to dialogue and encounter, but to mutual love. We must look ahead, and at what better point to begin than by affirming our faith together in the One True God, and to walk together with Him, as your Academy of Religion has chosen to do. Allow me for a moment to express my warmest thanks to you all, and especially to those of you who are officers of this Academy.

The Sacred Books themselves exhort us to set out resolutely on the open roads of encounter; they speak to each of us who consider the corner-stone of our religious encounter to be Abrahamic faith in the One God. Let us reflect again, with joy, on some of the most positive and encouraging of these texts.

Israel rejoices in the title "the People of God", segullah, and it is in no way my intention to diminish this honor given to it by the Eternal God. At the same time the prophets did not cease to urge them not only to respect those "timentes Deum, the worshippers of God", to whom the New Testament refers (e.g. Acts 16), but to remind them that they are called to fulfil the mission of Abraham of whom God said: "I have appointed you to be father of many nations"(Gen. 17:4) (Rom. 4:17). It is perhaps in the prophecies of Isaiah that this theme is carried furthest: "When that day comes Israel shall rank with Egypt and Assyria, those three, and shall be a blessing in the centre of the world. So the Lord of Hosts will bless them: A blessing be upon Egypt my people, upon Assyria the work of my hands, and upon Israel my possession"(Is. 19: 24-25). And, in his glorious vision of the future, he continues with joyful certainty: "Enlarge the limits of your home, spread wide the curtains of your tent; let out its ropes to the full ..." (Is. 54:2). The book of the prophet Jonah, vividly and with gentle irony, presents the Eternal God as desiring the salvation of all peoples, even those at enmity with Israel, and portrays Him as using an Israelite as the instrument to express this, putting Himself in dispute with the Israelite in order to combat Israel's temptation to isolationism.

The robust monotheism of Islām is well-known. It leads the Muslims to reject Christian belief in the Trinity, in the Incarnation of the Word of God, and in salvation through the mediation of Christ. They do not accept the complete Bible, judging there to be falsifications and distortions in it. yet they consider Christians as faithful monotheists according to the faith of Abraham, and use expressions in their regard which I should like to quote here: "Invite (all) to the Way of your lord with wisdom and beautiful preaching; and argue with them in ways that are best and most gracious: for your Lord knows best who have strayed from His path and who receive guidance" (Qur'ān, Sūrah XVI: 125). Again: "Those who believe (in the Qur'ān), and those who follow the Jewish (scriptures), and the Christians and the Sabians, and who believe in God and the Last Day, and work righteousness, shall have their reward with their lord; on them shall be no fear, nor shall they grieve" (Qur'ān, Sūrah II: 62).

Almost as a logical consequence of these assertions, the Qur'an also has these others: "If God had so willed, He would have made you a single people, but (His plan is) to test you in what He has given you: to strive as in a race in all virtues. The goal of you all is to God; it is He that will show you the truth of matters in which you dispute" (Qur'ān, Sūrah V:51); "... For us (is the responsibility for) our deeds, and for you for your deeds. There is no contention between us and you. God will bring us together, and to Him is (our— final goal" (Qur'ān, Sūrah XLII:15); "To each is a goal to which God turns him; then strive together (as in a race) towards all that is good, Wheresoever you are, God will bring you together. For God has power over all things" (Qur'ān, Sūrah II:148).

There may be those who object that some of these verses are abrogated by a particular type of exegesis. I would reply to them, if it were necessary, that there is a wider exegesis that is no less orthodox and that according to this exegesis the abrogation theory only applies to verses of a normative nature considered in strict relationship to precise factual events. [Editor's note at the end].

When we come to Christianity we see that in principle Christian doctrine, as seen especially in the Gospels, is unequivocally open to those having faith in the God of Abraham. In fact, however, there have been, on the part of Christians and the Churches, deplorable instances of intolerance and persecution that were in direct contrast with the doctrine of Christ. As I said regarding Judaism and Islām, even though I feel deep sorrow (indeed, I would say deep shame) for what has happened — and let us pray that it may never happen again — I am convinced that the best way to make amends for the past is to renew our minds and hearts in that spirit of love which is at the very foundation of our faith and to strive in this spirit with all our strength. Men like Pope John XXIII, like Paul VI and John Paul II, scholars like Jules Isaac, Massignon, Cardinal Bea and thousands of others from each of our monotheistic religions, have shown us the road we should walk.

The Second Vatican Council expressed clearly and authoritatively the attitude that we Catholics should have in regard to our Jewish and Muslim brothers and sisters. If I read these texts, taken from the Second Vatican Council's Declaration *Nostra Aetate*, I do not think further words will be necessary. Here is what is said on the relation of the Church to the Jewish faith: "As this Council searches into the mystery of the Church, it recalls the spiritual bond linking the people of the New Covenant with Abraham's stock. (*N. 4*)

For the Church of Christ acknowledges that, according to the mystery of God's saving design, the beginnings of her faith and her election are already found among the patriarchs, Moses, and the

5

prophets. She professes that all who believe in Christ, Abraham's sons according to faith (cf. Gal. 3:7), are included in the same patriarch's call, and likewise that the salvation of the Church was mystically foreshadowed by the chosen people's exodus from the land of bondage. (*N. 2*)

The Church, therefore, cannot forget that she received the revelation of the Old Testament through the people with whom God in his inexpressible mercy deigned to establish the Ancient Covenant. Nor can she forget that she draws sustenance from the root of that good olive tree onto which have been grafted the wild olive branches of the Gentiles (cf. Rom. 11: 17-24). Indeed, the Church believes that by His cross Christ, our Peace, reconciled Jew and Gentile, making them both one in Himself (cf. Eph 2: 14-16).

Also the Church ever keeps in mind the words of the Apostle about his kinsmen, "who have the adoption as sons, and the glory from the covenant and the legislation and the worship and the promises; who have the fathers, and from whom is Christ according to the flesh"(Rom. 9:4-5), the son of the Virgin Mary. The Church recalls too that from the Jewish people sprang the apostles, her foundations, stones and pillars, as well as most of the early disciples who proclaimed Christ to the world.

Since the spiritual patrimony common to Christians and Jews is thus so great, this sacred Council wishes to foster and recommend that mutual understanding and respect which is the fruit above all of biblical and theological studies, and of brotherly dialogues."

And here is what is said in the same document regarding the relationship of the Catholic Church to the Muslims: "Upon the Muslims, too, the Church looks with esteem. They adore one God, living and enduring, merciful and all-powerful, Maker of heaven and earth and Speaker to men. They strive to submit wholeheartedly even to His inscrutable decrees, just as did Abraham, with whom the Islamic faith is pleased to associate itself. Though they do not acknowledge Jesus as God, they revere Him as a prophet. They also honor Mary, His virgin mother; at times they call on her, too, with devotion. In addition they await the day of judgement when God will give each man his due after raising him up. Consequently, they prize the moral life, and give worship to God especially through prayer, almsgiving, and fasting.

Although in the course of the centuries many quarrels and hostilities have arisen between Christians and Muslims, this most sacred Council urges all to forget the past and to strive sincerely for mutual understanding. On behalf of all mankind, let them make common cause of safeguarding and fostering social justice, moral values, peace and freedom". (*N. 3*)

6

2. The enormous spiritual force of the great religions that are united in the faith of Abraham.

If we now come to consider from the point of view of their relations with the world of today the three great religions of Judaism, Christianity and Islām, we can recognize the enormous impact they could have on the world. The modern world, even if it has been enriched with many exterior values (which one would not wish to despise in any way) has nevertheless become spititually impoverished to a disturbing degree. The Orientals would say: it has become a world "of having" at the expense of the world "of being". One can observe that while the means for securing well-being and an easier, more comfortable and pleasurable existence have increased, human happiness has not automatically increased; indeed, in many cases it has diminished to a preoccupying extent. One of the reasons for this human condition of dissatisfaction (to which we could add the wide area of problems stretching from misery to injustice, to hatred, to denial of liberty), indeed, we would say the fundamental reason from which man's profound unease and dissatisfaction and those other problems follow is that the world of today has, to a great extent, turned away from God and from His Law, and considers that it is sufficient to itself.

In a world where "God is absent" man finds himself fearfully isolated and, as it were, abandoned down a blind alley. Only in God, the God of Abraham, is man able to find his true measure, and to live his existence in time to its fulness, opening himself to the certainty of eternal life. "When I turn away from you," says Juda Halevy in his poem, *Kuzari* "although I live, I am dead; but when I draw near to you, even if dead I am alive". In his book *The Primal Vision,* John Taylor gives this view of the African peoples: "The African myth does not tell of men driven from Paradise, but of God disappearing from the world".

While Judaism, Christianity and Islam are at one in their affirmation that God is "Wholly-Other", they are also agreed that He is the "Wholly-Near". As a powerful Muslim expression puts it, God is closer to man than his own jugular vein. Man is not a lost and practically useless fragment of the cosmos, but a creature of God, made in His image and consequently worthy of respect and love. Man is called to live a moral life, bound to his fellow human beings by the ideal of peace and brotherhood. If man gives way to the temptation of "liberating" himself from God, he ends by becoming the slave of those petty but terrible "gods" called power, wealth, pleasure, etc.; only too often these "gods", these "idols", hide under noble names such as progress, social concern, and even freedom. Yet only as a creature of God does man receive the right to subject the earth, to till it and keep it (le'avdàh welesharah)

(Gen. 2:15); the Qur'ān says that creation is subject to man because he is the representative of God (His khalīfah).

All of us here feel the awesome but marvelous responsibility of being "friends of God" and we are sure that by being such we are thereby authentic friends of our fellow men. We have neer separated, and even less have we seen an opposition, between the world as such and the religious world. We have never seen them as two separate kingdoms; they both come from God! "The word 'methistemi', in the sense of transference out of one realm into another, is only once used in the New Testament (Col. 1: 13). The typical New Testament word is 'metanoia', which means turning about. The emphasis is entirely on a change of direction, not on a change of position" (John Taylor).

I think it would be useful here to recall the words of Martin Buber: "One does not find God if one remains in the world. One does not find God if one goes out of the world ... Certainly, God is the "Wholly-Other", but He is also the "Wholly-Same", the all present. He is indeed the 'mysterium tremendum' at the sight of whom we are terrified, but He is also the mystery of presence who is closer to me than myself". William Temple once made this seemingly paradoxical observation: "Christianity is the most materialistic of all relgions in the world. It does take the terrestrial realities seriously". The author is saying that it takes terrestrial reality seriously because it takes God seriously. I think the same could be said of the Jewish and Muslim faiths.

At this point I should like to make a personal observation that comes to me spontaneously from my work in the Vatican Secretariat for Non-Christians. Side by side with the Jews and Muslims, namely the brothers and sisters who share my personal adherence to the faith of Abraham, there exist millions of men and women (I do not hesitate to say hundreds of millions) belonging to non-Abrahamic religions — such as Hindus, Buddhists, Shintoists, Confucianists, etc. — whom I feel to be practically united to me by their belief in divine and religious values. There are others who state that "they have no religion" (as I have often heard young friends of mine say to me, be they from Hong-Kong, Singapore or Los Angeles. But if we push a little further we often find that what they mean is that they do not belong to a Christian Church, or that they are not part of what God called "His people", or that they are not part of the Ummah, or, in other words, that they do not belong to any religion organized as an institution. Yet they are often really and truly "friends of God", and thus in a way form part of our community of religious believers. Maritain said: "Men only become one by their spirit". I would say that around us and together with us there are millions of such men of the spirit. Sometimes they are of such spiritual depth that they give the impression of being "true mystics"; their eyes and hearts are turned towards the Eternal God.

This is a reality that gives us enormous encouragement. Not that it is our intention to form a stronger and more compact "front" to set against the "front" of the non-believers. No. This would be an offence against the God who loves us, all of us, and whom we would wish to see loved by all. We are happy because we see that the family of believers in God is a large one, and we pray to the Most High that all of humanity may come to be part of this family. Only He has the power to achieve it.

3. What should we do, as single believers or as communities of believers, in order that others may come to our faith or come close to it?

All of us here today are well aware that while we share a commitment to the faith of Abraham, there are nevertheless considerable differences in the way our three religions envisage the relation of God with man.

Judaism recognizes a covenant between God and his people; unlike the Christians, however, Judaism does not accept Jesus Christ as the Mediator between God and man. Islām, while recognizing Jesus as a prophet, does not accept Him as a Mediator. Indeed, a Muslim holds that he needs no intermediary between himself and God. Every Muslim believer addresses God without an intermediary, as is clearly expressed in the rites or the prayer ritual (Ṣalāh) and in those of the pilgrimage to Makkah.

Islām is, however, a "missionary" religion in which each of the faithful has the duty of proclaiming the message of God (da'wah). The Christian religion is likewise missionary, in which between God and man there exist bonds of filial love. While not excluding an openness to conversion, Judaism would not, I think, nromally consider itself missionary in the same sense. But whatever the difference in approach between our relgions, I would like to say just one thing on the matter of the proclaiming of the religious message: accepting the right of each of our religions of Abrahamic faith (and naturally, the right also of other religions) to proclaim their message freely, we must do it in such a way that the freedom of the other is always respected. God is a God of freedom and He does not ask for an adherence extorted by violence.

"Let the man who wants to follow me ..." was the formula used by Christ. He refused to invoke fire from heaven as some of his disciples one day asked Him to do; He said to them: "You do not know of what spirit you are". When he has honestly given witness to his faith and reached the frontier of the human conscience, the apostle (be he Christian, Muslim, or whatever) must leave to that conscience the full right of decision, excluding any form of constriction, be it open or hidden. There have been examples of the opposite in the past; it is better to put these behind us and not repeat them. The essential norm and condition for accepting a religion or not should be based on the human person's freedom of conscience.

My dear friends, there is not time for me to develop this point. I only mention in passing that the Declaration of Religious Freedom, published in 1965 after two years of intense debate and reflection, remains one of the major texts of the Second Vatican Council. It expresses clearly in what way the Church to which I belong is able to respect the freedom of other Churches and religions without thereby diminishing in any way her commitment to the faith of Abraham and the Gospel of Christ. I hardly need to add that in the United States this principle or religious freedom is well understood since the Founding Fathers, when framing the First Amendment in 1791, clearly affirmed the right of the person and of communities to the free exercise of religion in society.

But let me return to our main discourse. We do, I believe, have two clear obligations to men and women who do not share our Abrahamic faith or who have no religious faith at all. And it seems to me that these duties could be accepted and practised not only by those of us who are Christians, but also by our Jewish and Muslim brothers:

a) The first duty is to open the way to a clear and loyal dialogue with all of our fellow men. To open does not, of course, mean to impose! The substance of the book of Martin Buber, "Life in Dialogue", from which I quoted above, is summed up in the phrase: "In the beginning there is relationship". This reminds me of two proverbs on a similar theme. One is the Arab proverb: "Man is the enemy of what he does not know," and the other is an African proverb of the Wolof people which says: "When you begin by dialogue, you reach a solution".

Between our religions there have been too many periods of separation and silence. Our Vatican Secretariats, one for Christian Unity, another for Non-Christians (with two Commissions, one for relations with Judaism, the other for relations with Islam, both of them established on the same day, 22nd October 1974), another Secretariat for Non-Believers, together with the World Council of Churches and so many other International Organizations (among which I limit myself to mentioning the Kennedy Institute, the Interreligous Peace Colloquium that is our host, the Standige Konferenz von Juden, Christen und Muslims in Europa, etc), are all bearing fruit in the exchange of ideas and in friendship. As one of the final statements of the Broumana Colloquium, organized by the World Council of Churches in 1972, put it: "The common search for the will of God is growing."

What will be the fruit of these increased meetings and dialogues? It is difficult to say. What is certain is that they are not without value. As Fr. Michel Lelong has observed in his recent book, *"Deux fidelitiés, une espérance,"* "However serious political conflicts may be, it is

10

unacceptable that faith in God should aggravate them". Even if the religions themselves provide no solution, they must nevertheless always be elements helping towards true and just peace.

b) The second duty is to do what can be done so that those who are believers in the One God may attract and inspire others, and especially non-believers, to find faith in Him. It can never be repeated sufficiently that it is not a question of making "a solid front of believers against unbelievers". That would, basically, damage the very spirit of religion itself. The dialogues and the encounter of our three religions of Abrahamic faith, and of these with other religions, must be a joining of hearts before becoming a meeting of minds.

The Qur'ān reminds the Muslims that "the closest in friendship are those who are not puffed up with pride"(Sūrah V:82), and "Be courteous when your argue with the people of the Book" (Sūrah XXIX: 46). A famous hadīth says: "No one among you will be a true believer as long as he does not desire for his brother what he desires for himself." As far as Christians are concerned, St. Paul warns us: "Let us cease judging one another" (Rom. 14:13), and again: "Leave no claim outstanding against you, except of mutual love" (Rom. 13:8).

I should like to close with a final wish, a final hope. But rather than doing this with my own pedestrian words, let me quote to you from three different sources, each of them touching different aspects of our theme.

Firstly, a rabbinical teaching: "What in all of human speech is the most fundamental phrase? I did not hesitate for a moment before crying out with all my voice: 'Listen, Israel: the Eternal is our God, the Eternal is One'! Is not this the highest phrase of all, the phrase without equal in heaven and on earth? Then I asked myself: but what in this sublime phrase is the most fundamental word? I replied to myself that without any doubt it is the word 'ekhad', meaning one. Finally, I asked myself: And of all the words in human speech, which would be the most eminent among those whose letters, when added together, have the same numerical value as the holy word 'ekhad', whose value is thirteen? I did not have to search for long: at my fingertips, deep in my heart, at the centre of my soul, there was the word 'ahavah': love".

Secondly, a poem by the Senegalese poet and journalist Niaky Barry. It expresses the desire to draw together, at least in the heart, our religions of Abrahamic faith together with the other religions of mankind. I shall quote it in French and then hazard a translation in English:

"*Ah, frère de l'universel — c'est dans le noyau central de ton âme — que j'érigerai le Sanctuaire du Dieu Ultime — d'où Synagogue, Temple, Eglise et Mosquée — seront en harmonie — dans les flots mouvants do ton élan vers l'Infini*".

"Ah, brother of all things — it is in the central reaches of your soul — that I will build the Sactuary of the Everlasting God — where Synagogue, Temple, Church and Mosque — will dwell in harmony — amidst the surging waves of your longing and search for the Infinite".

Thirdly and lastly, a poem by Edwin Markham. In his desire to unite all in understanding and brotherhood, he has written these words, with which I close:

He drew a circle that shut me out,
Heretic, rebel, a thing to flout.
But love and I had the wit to win;
We drew a circle that took him in.

Thank you.

Editor's Note:

No Muslim thinker has claimed that any exegesis can or did "abrogate" any verse of the Qur'ān. The Cardinal must have therefore meant the supplanting of one exegesis with another in somebody's mind. However, because of the frozenness of Arabic lexicography and syntax since the revelation of the Qur'ān, exegesis can indeed establish its conclusions critically.

Topic I
THE OTHER FAITHS
CHAPTER 2
ISLAM AND CHRISTIANITY IN THE PERSPECTIVE OF JUDAISM

Michael Wyschogrod
Professor of Philosophy
Baruch College, City University of New York

Judaism's view of Christianity and Islām is a function of its understanding of itself. The term "Judaism" is itself problematic in the light of traditional Jewish self-understanding. The term implies the existence of a set of beliefs and practices which constitute Judaism and adherence to which makes someone into a Jew. The term "Judaism" does not translate any classical Hebrew term. The reason for this is that the critical term in classical Jewish self-understanding is not Judaism (though we cannot avoid using the term) but Israel and the Torah. Israel is the people that is descended from Abraham, Isaac and Jacob and that has been chosen to serve as God's people and as a blessing to all of humanity (Gen. 12:3). The Torah is the divinely revealed teaching that explains the origins and nature of Israel and of the commandments God has addressed to his people. The Torah and Israel are therefore closely related: the Torah as command is addressed not to all of humanity but only to Israel and Israel is a people only because of the covenant to which the Torah testifies. No Judaism is therefore possible without the people of Israel. But who is the people of Israel?

The people of Israel are the descendants of Abraham, Isaac and Jacob. God could have chosen a community of faith to serve as his people (which is what he did, in the view of the Church, when he constituted it as the New Israel). God could have chosen a group not constituted by faith but by action: those who acted in a certain way would then have been members of the chosen people. Or he could have not chosen any one people but all of humanity without any invidious distinctions. But, in his sovereignty, God did not choose any of these options. Instead, he addressed Abraham, Isaac and Jacob and established a special relationship with them. This human family defined

13

in terms of descent from the patriarchs became the Jewish people. Judaism is therefore not a matter of faith. A Jew who lacks faith or who acts contrary to the commandments of the Torah is therefore a sinning Jew. But he remains a Jew and the fact is that all Jews are, to a greater or lesser extent, sinning Jews. Ontologically, in terms of what he is, the Jew is a Jew because of descent from the patriarchs.

And yet, conversion to Judaism is possible. That it is possible is not very obvious. From the point of view of simple common sense, it ought not to be possible. One cannot convert to being someone's descendant. In many legal systems, adoption becomes a method whereby someone who is not a physical descendant legally becomes one. But it is worth noting that Jewish law does not know of adoption. If conversion to Judaism is possible — as it is — it becomes a possibility by means of a kind of miracle. The convert miraculously becomes seed of Abraham, Isaac and Jacob. And this ought not to be interpreted too spiritually. In the rabbinic view, a son and mother who convert may marry without violating the biblical prohibition against incest (though it becomes rabinically prohibited) because by converting they have been born again and are therefore no longer mother and son. The rebirth in question can hardly be a purely spiritual one because in a purely spiritual rebirth, as in Christian baptism, the biological bond between mother and son is not severed. It is for this reason that no Christian author known to me entertains the possibility that baptism of mother and son produces a rebirth which cancels the incest prohibition between them. But in Jewish conversion, something quasi-biological occurs and it is for this reason that the possibility of conversion does not undermine Jewish self-understanding in terms of descent from Abraham.

If the Torah is the system of God's demands addressed to Israel, where do other nations stand? The election of Israel imposes on this people a special set of commands to which it, and only it, is called to obedience. But God is not indifferent to the faith and conduct of other peoples either. These, in view of the rabbis, are bound by the Noachide commandments which the rabbis infer from Gen. 9 and which exclude idolatry, murder, theft, incest, roughly corresponding to the natural moral law. A gentile who fulfills these commands secures for himself a place in the world to come. Judaism therefore does not teach that only its adherents can be "saved" or that it is the only path to "salvation". Judaism is the set of demands God makes of the Jewish people and since those demands are not easy to fulfill, and since it is possible to obtain a place in the world to come without being a Jew, there is a *prima facie* case to be made against encouraging gentiles to convert to Judaism. And indeed that has been the general Jewish attitude toward converts. They are not encouraged to convert but told that God does not want all of the human family to follow the same rules and that, as gentiles, they please God most adequately by fulfilling the Noachide commandments. Only when the potential convert persists in his search and insists on becoming a Jew is he circumcised (if male) and required to immerse himself in the *Mikvah* (ritual bath) from which, if he has committed himself to the observance of the Torah, does he emerge as a full-fledged Jew.

The Jewish view of Christianity and Islâm must therefore be understood in the context of Judaism's understanding of itself. Because Judaism is not seen as the "right" religion for everyone, it is self-evident that the other religions have a right to exist provided they do not violate one or another of the Noachide commandments. In the case of Islâm and because of its supremely monotheistic orientation, Judaism has had no difficulty in recognizing it as a valid expression of gentile religiosity. In the case of Christianity the matter becomes more complex. The root of the difficulty is the doctrine of the Trinity. As formulated in the Nicene Creed which speaks of the Son who was "begotten, not made" and "of one essence with the Father", the question arises whether Christianity is, in fact, a break with monotheism and therefore in violation of the Noachide prohibition against idolatry. Medieval rabbis were divided over the answer to this question. The accepted view was that Christianity did not constitute idolatry for gentiles. The doctrine of the Trinity weakened but did not fatally injure the oneness of God. Nevertheless, it was held that for a Jew to hold to the doctrine of the Trinity would constitute idolatry. This descrepancy was to be understood in terms of a difference in the standard of monotheism as applicable to Jews and to gentiles. It is the Torah which defines what sort of belief constitutes idolatry for Jews and what sort of belief constitutes idolatry for gentiles. The Jewish standards are more stringent (as in many other requirements) than those applicable to gentiles so that one and the same belief can constitute idolatry for Jews and not for gentiles. And this is, in fact, the case with regard to the Trinity.

In the case of Islâm, there is no such problem with regard to monotheism. But here another problem arises which is also quite serious. Whatever problem Judaism may have with Christianity with respect to the Trinity, there remains one extremely important bond: they both revere the Hebrew Bible as the word of God. There are, of course, serious differences of interpretation, most notably perhaps the Christian belief that many passages in the Hebrew Bible refer to ("foreshadow" is the commonly used term) the life and death of Jesus of Nazareth. And there are other ways in which traditional Christian hermeneutics of the Hebrew Bible differs from Jewish understanding. Nevertheless, the text of the Hebrew Bible is accepted by Christians as divinely inspired. Muslims, on the other hand, do not go so far. While they accept much from the Hebrew Bible, they also believe that serious distortions have crept into the Hebrew text, distortions mainly aiming to justify the Jewish version of things. While in a general way Islām accepts the incidents and teachings of the Hebrew Bible, it cannot be said that there is a common Scripture as there is with Christianity. Maimonides, in fact, attaches so much importance to this difference that he permits Torah to be taught to Christians but not to Muslims. Since the difference between Judaism and Christianity is the interpretation of the Hebrew Bible, teaching the Jewish interpretation to Christians may serve to correct the Christian misinterpretation. But with Muslims it is not a matter of a difference of interpretation of a shared text but a rejection by Muslims of the Hebrew Bible as transmitted in Judaism. Since they do not accept the text, Maimonides holds that Muslims may not be taught Torah as there is little chance of coming to any sort of agreement.

While it would be wrong to attach too much importance to this particular ruling of Maimonides both because it is one man's opinion and not a very central part of Maimonides' thinking at that, it is interesting to note the symmetry of the Jewish-Christian and Jewish-Muslim relationship. Each has one important plus and one important minus. With Christianity there is the important advantage of the common Scripture but there is the problem of the Trinity. With Islām, there is the advantage of no impairment of monotheism but there is the problem of the absence of a common Scripture. It is difficult to say which relationship, on balance, is the easier. Perhaps it should also be mentioned that the charge of being responsible for the death of Jesus and therefore of deicide was never raised in Islām and that this also contributes to a less tense relationship with Islām. And it is generally held that while deprivation of the human rights of Jews was by no means unknown in the Muslim world (at least as measured by contemporary standards), it did not generally reach the severity that this form of human prejudice did in the Christian world. It is not necessary to interpret Jewish existence in the Muslim world as an uninterrupted exercise in mutual cordiality to recognize that the virulent anti-semitism that has infected much of Christendom cannot be easily found in the Muslim sphere.

Up to this point, the Jewish evaluation of Christianity and Islām has been discussed from the point of view of Judaism's understanding of the Noachide commandments which it considers obligatory for gentiles and by means of which it measures any religion or ideology adopted by gentiles. Seen from this point of view, a gentile religion which made no reference to Jewish sacred history could pass muster quite adequately. But it is significant, of course, that both Christianity and Islām are not at all oblivious to God's intervention in human affairs through the history of Israel. To a significant extent, Christianity and Islām have absorbed and propagated concepts that first arose in Israel's religious history and which would have remained Israel's alone were they not spread throughout the world by Judaism's two daughter religions. These two religions — Christianity and Islām — therefore stand in a special relationship to Judaism and Judaism stands in a special relationship to them. This was clearly recognized by Judaism almost from the very inception of these two religions. It is for this reason that Maimonides, in a well-known passage, attributes an important place in God's plan of salvation to Christianity and Islām. He writes:

But it is beyond the human mind to fathom the designs of the Creator; for our ways are not His ways, neither are our thoughts His thoughts. All these matters relating to Jesus of Nazareth and the Ishmaelite (Muḥammad) who came after him, only served to clear the way for King Messiah, to prepare the whole world to worship God with one accord, as it is written "For then will I turn to the peoples a pure language, that they may all call upon the name of the Lord to serve Him with one consent" (Zeph. 3:9). Thus the messianic hope, the Torah, and the commandments have become familiar topics — topics of conversation (among the inhabitants) of the far isles and many peoples, uncircumcised of heart and flesh." (The Code of Maimonides, The Book of Judges, tr. Abraham M. Hershman, Yale University Press, 1949, p. XXIII).

Through Judaism and Islām, messianic thinking has entered into the consciousness of peoples who would otherwise have had no understanding whatsoever of this profoundly Jewish expectation. Since it is clear to Maimonides that the redemption that awaits Israel at the end of time will be accompanied by the redemption of the rest of humanity, the spread of messianism in its Christian and Muslim forms is an integral part of the movement of history according to God's plan.

If Judaism does not adopt a missionary stance toward Christians and Muslims, it does not do so because it does not believe it to be God's will that all of humanity become Jewish. It has often been overlooked that this does not rule out a Noachide mission to gentiles. Because all of humanity is obligated to live up to the demands of the Noachide covenant which follows the Flood as reported in Genesis, it would seem obvious that it is Israel's task, as the people to whom the Torah was entrusted, to propagate knowledge of this covenant among the peoples. Furthermore, Israel's own election is not an end in itself but has as its goal the blessing of all humanity (Gen. 12:3). Only when man's disobedience seemed to frustrate God's original plan (Gen. 6:6) did he decide to concentrate his pedagogy on one of the human families apparently hoping that if he succeeds with this one group, its example

17

will serve to educate the rest of humanity to live in accordance with God's will. And if Israel has also proven less than fully equal to the task demanded of it, its failures have interfered with the redemption of all of humanity and not only its own redemption.

To charge Israel with an exclusionary, even racist, theology, is therefore a profound distortion of Israel's faith. That God elected a human family of the flesh was His sovereign prerogative. In spite of the hereditary nature of this election, conversion to Judaism is possible for all those who sincerely desire it. The very fact that it is possible, even if not encouraged, emphasizes the complex and not completely hereditary nature of this election. And above all, by accepting its election, Israel commits itself to a more difficult life of obedience than is required of any other people. It is true that in spite of all the suffering that has accrued to Israel because of its election, Israel has developed a certain pride because of its election and its service. Doubtless, at times this has exceeded the bounds of the permissible. But what could be expected of a people that has kept the faith in spite of superhuman obstacles and because of it brought a large segment of humanity under the wings of the divine presence?

The demand of the hour is a drawing together of all those whose lives are led under the judgment of the God of Abraham. For the children of Abraham to learn to recognize the presence of the patriarch in the adherents of the other Abrahamic faiths is the demand of the teacher of Beer-Sheva. We ought not to reject that demand.

CHAPTER 3
JUDAISM AND ISLĀM IN THE PERSPECTIVE OF CHRISTIANITY

Krister Stendahl

Dean of the Divinity School, Harvard University

The ground rules for viewing other traditions and their adherents are simple and far-reaching: Compare equal to equal — and allow others to define themselves.

The first rule is obvious. Yet the apologist in us often makes it too tempting to compare one's own tradition in its ideal form with the actual — or even especially bad — forms of the other. For example, Christians may flatter themselves with being the religion of love and peace over against Jewish legalism or Muslim belligerence. As if the Christian history had been so peaceful and loving, or as if Judaism and Islām did not know of compassionate love and manifestations of Shalom/Salām.

The second rule guards against a more subtle, but equally self-serving habit of religious folk. I refer to the habit of defining the other's religion in a manner enhancing one's own value and superiority. Or, when there are attempts at a positive evaluation of the other, then we are drawn to those elements in the other's religion which are most attractive to us since they are similar to our own tradition. Thus we Christians tend to construct a Christianized form of the other's tradition, paying little attention to how the other sees and experiences, or to what is central and what is peripheral to that tradition for its adherents.

It is important to recognize that also this latter habit, with its positive intentions, is distorting in a self-serving manner. For it suggests that we can only be positive by recognizing in others what we like in ourselves. The ultimate expression of this attitude is the term "anonymous Christians" for those of other relgions that we approve of, i.e. we can only express our approval by claiming that they are like us — although "anonymously". For contrast, it may be significant to remember that the equivalent term in Judaism is "righteous Gentiles," i.e., a clear recognition that the other is not like oneself — yet can be right and even righteous in the eyes of God.

But I have not been asked to compare religions, but rather to give a Christian view of Judaism and Islām. Even so, I do not understand that assignment to give me dispensation from the above-mentioned laws of comparative religion. On the contrary, a Christian view of Judaism and Islām must be continually corrected by the listening, by the dialogue in which we can find out whether we have understood or misrepresented the other. If we do not observe that law we are in danger of breaking the precious commandment: Thou shalt not bear false witness against your neighbor.

In such a continuous process it often becomes clear that there is a great deal of asymmetry between religions — and even between "the three religions of the Book." For example, it is often said that an understanding of Judaism is essential for Christianity — but that no such understanding of Christianity is *essential* for Judaism. From a historical perspective of development that may be true, since Christianity grew out of Judaism and the Jewish Scriptures became part of the Christian Bible, while Judaism had its own integrity of development. When Christians have difficulties with that asymmetry, and with the Jewish desire to be left alone, they should be reminded of how completely they have neglected the theological and religious insights and challenges of Islām.

Such a developmental pattern of Christian thought in its more popular form rests on the feeling that the later is the better, the New Testament is superior to the Old, etc. ... without granting Islām the logical status of being even "newer." And on all levels such a pattern leads to one of the attitudes which have come to have dire results in human history. I have in mind the habit of having the other play an inferior, negative or even satanic role in one's own pattern of salvation. As to Jewish-Christian relations, this can be seen already in the Gospel of John, where "Jews" have already become a symbol for satanic un-faith. It could be said that the ultimate violence against the other is to use them as negative symbols in one's own system.

It is actually against such attitudes of conceit that Paul is warning Gentile Christians in Rom. 11:11-36 — suggesting a mysterious co-existence between Church and Israel side by side until the eschaton when Israel's salvation is assured on her own terms — "for the gifts and the call of God are irrevocable."

The Jewish thinker Maimonides gives another example of "a positive role for the other" when he sees Christianity and Islām as the positive bearers of Torah to the Gentile world, i.e. a grateful recognition of the function of the other.

The historical perspective out of which the above reflections grow may, however, not be the only or the most authentic perspective, once we allow the other to define herself. From a historical perspective Islām "begins" in the seventh century of the Christian era. But such is a modern historical perception. If I understand it right, for Islām Muḥammad is not the originator of a religion but a prophet in continuity. Not only is there the common roots of our three faiths in Abraham, but Islām is grounded in eternity — as is Christianity in the pre-existent Logos, and Judaism in the beginning when God created the world on the model of the week with the Sabbath rest on the Seventh Day.

From such a theological perspective it is not easy to find the right order for listing the three. If I say "Judaism-Christianity-Islām", the implication is that of developmental history. It may be wise to question that order, so natural to the academic community and those conditioned by it. Perhaps the best way of doing that is to use the good old alphabet — which in English would give us "Christianity-Islām-Judaism."

Let me conclude these reflections with three observations as to the value, perhaps even imperative of a tri-partite dialogue between the Three.

A deepened reflection of our common bond in Abraham could open up new vistas. As a student of the Christian Bible, I am, for example, struck by the manner in which the apostle Paul reaches back just to Abraham as he seeks roots for his mission to the Gentiles. I, for one, would like to explore this bond in a deeper tri-partite way, i.e. not only with Israel but also with Islām.

Secondly, I am painfully aware of the persistent streak of violence that has plagued Christianity's history in the world — beautiful love-language notwithstanding. I feel an urgent need of an open dialgue with Islām and Judaism where the topic could be: What resources exist in our respective traditions that can serve as counterbalance to that violence of words and deeds which may be rooted in a symbol system where salvation is victory — and hence, there are the vanquished.

Finally, more attention should perhaps be given to that transcendence of limits of time and space and labels for which the mystics stand, mystics with which all our traditions have been blest ...

CHAPTER 4
JUDAISM AND CHRISTIANITY IN THE
PERSPECTIVE OF ISLĀM

Muḥammad 'Abd al Ra'ūf
Islamic Center of Washington, D.C.

I. Foreword

We meet today in a climate of tension caused by recent events in Iran. The whole world erupted in protests and appeals. The Pope sent an emissary to the Iranian ruler appealing for the release of those taken as hostages at the embassy of the United States in Tehran. The Security Council of the United Nations took a unanimous resolution calling for the immediate release of those hostages. Similar appeals and voices of condemnation are heard aloud elsewhere.

We do not by any means advocate or even condone the practice of taking hostages as a measure of attaining legitimate aspiration; but the recent events in Iran have aroused in us, as well as in any serious and honest humans, deep reflections— nay anxieties — over past events of recent history. For decades the Muslims of Iran were tyrannized over by an inhuman dictatorship which slaughtered, tortured and maimed them with the full blessing — even collaboration — of the West. Palestinians were driven from their own home *en masse* by Zionists or Western Jews seeking to capture a land and empty it of its people in order to repopulate it by strangers. The process by which this genocide has been accomplished was cultural and political, as well as military. After massacring inhabitants and dumping their bodies in the village well (as happened at Deir Yasin), or killing a few and terrorizing the rest and ordering them out of their homes and lands which they had occupied for millennia (as happened and continues to happen every day throughout Palestine), every Arab vestige in the village is wiped out. Tens and tens of thousands of humans have been killed, tortured or maimed while the Christian West furnished all the political and economic support, and supplied the arms and munitions needed by the perpetrators of genocide. Southern Lebanon's innocent citizens have been bombarded by the most destructive weapons — napalm and cluster bombs — generously given by a nation committed to the so-called Judeo-Christian moral tradition. Moreover, America has spared nothing in its arsenal which it did not give to the perpetrators of these crimes so as to make them invincible even if three quarters of the earth stood against them. Millions of Muslims in the Philippines, Ethiopia, Eritrea, Somalia, Thailand, Burma, India, Afghanistan, and in many other places are rendered homeless or killed or maimed, either by Christians or by others who are helped, kept in power and armed by Christians. Muslim minorities everywhere are struggling to survive under oppressive regimes that seek to liquidate them.

In all these tragic happenings, no similar protest is heard. No outcry for the violation of human rights. No support for the victims is contemplated except what may enhance the public image of the West. Indeed, the veto is used to abort any world condemnation in the United Nations. Where was, and where is the human conscience of the West that is outraged today at Iran's seizure of the hostages? What does its silence—nay, collaboration—yesterday, and outcry today tell us about its humanity? Again, we should like to stress that we disagree with the method of taking an innocent human being a hostage. But are the life and suffering of those millions of Muslims not equally worthy of concern?

This is not unrelated to my theme, but is most germane to it. For I maintain that it is the deepest convictions entertained deliberately and consciously, or held in the subconscious by indoctrination in childhood, that make humans behave as they do, whether individually or collectively; and these convictions are certainly generated by religious doctrine, by faith and its attitude to others.

II. Three levels of Discourse

First, being the youngest of the world religions, and, in its self-understanding, intended to be the religion of all humans, Islām had to relate itself to the religions of mankind, and through them to humanity. Second, being a reaffirmation and re-crystallization of the Semitic religious tradition, Islām had to relate itself to all Semitic religions, i.e., to its predecessors within that tradition. Thirdly, Islām also related itself to Judaism and Christianity in the most intimate way because, again in its self-understanding, it saw itself standing in great affinity with them. Consequently, Islām relates itself to Jews and Christians on all three levels: As humans, as heirs of the Semitic religious tradition, and as Jews and Christians. This relationship was on this account built into Islām's very nature and core. There is no Islām without it, as we shall see in the sequel.

24

A. The Human or Universal Level

Islam affirms the existence of primordial, natural religion, a genuine *religio naturalis*, which is the gift of God to all humans. It is called *dīn al fiṭrah*, or the religion of nature or creation. All humans are endowed with it without exception; for it comes to them at birth. It is an integral part of their personality, of their very being. God called this natural religion "His own religion" and commanded all humans to honor and belong to it. "Turn your face to the primordial religion, the religion in which God created all humans. That is the immutable pattern of God" (Qur'ān 30:30). Islām identified this *Ur-Religion* as the endowment of reason and understanding, of the critical faculties. "Only those with knowledge will reason out and understand it" (Qur'ān 29:43). Islām declared the human senses as avenues of knowledge (Qur'ān 90:8-10; 2:269); of the tools of knowledge such as language and writing (Qur'ān 96:1-5; 68:1). All these are "perfections" which God created, which He bestowed, to the end that humans make themselves felicitous by their use. The use of all these faculties or perfections God commanded, must be responsible; i.e., it must lead to the religion of God whose observance is felicity. "Hearing, seeing, and understanding — [all faculties of knowing] must be responsible" (Qur'ān 17:36).

The content of natural religion is universally imperative. All humans ought to fulfill it since they have been equipped at birth with all that is required to know it. As such it constitutes their *raison d'être*. Its first component is the recognition that God is indeed God; that no one else is God. The rest of its content revolves around the creature's creatureliness *vis-à-vis* the Creator, a relationship which can be none other than worship and service. "I have not created humans or jinn but to serve Me" (Qur'ān 51:56) It is the observance of His patterns which are knowable by reason with which He equipped all humans. No human may therefore be justified in his *kufr*, or unGodliness. And no human may be excused for falling into *shirk* or polytheism. Recognition and hence acknowledgment of God as God is everybody's business, everybody's prerogative, everybody's possibility, and everybody's supreme duty. Islām has no countenance for those religions or theories which discriminate between humans at birth, deeming some capable and others incapable by nature of knowing the one God. With such doctrines, the said religions or theories absolve those whom they declare incapable of the supreme duty of acknowledge and worshipping the one God. They thus rob them of their humanity. In fact, any tolerance or leniency on this point is tantamount to denying the normativeness of the divine Unity, and hence to sharing in the failure. Natural religion is absolutely normative for all humans. By definition, it admits of no exception. While it may not coerce anyone into observing its tenets, it is categorically opposed to, and necessarily condemning of, those who violate them, or permit or tolerate their violation. It is necessarily proselytizing and missionary. Otherwise it would not be consistent with itself. Islām identified itself with the religion of nature (Qur'ān 2:19). God called it "the religion" and declared it His own (Qur'ān 2:132). It therefore presents its case as a demand of nature, a necessary requisite of reason, a critical truth (Qur'ān 22:78).

The universalism of *religio naturalis* is further buttressed by Islām's understanding of history. Islām affirms that God did not leave mankind entirely to its own resources in the matter of acknowledging Him as God and Creator. In His mercy, He sent prophets to convey to them His divine message that they owe religion to God alone. "There is no people but unto them We sent a messenger... There is no people but We made them recipients of the message that they owe service to God and avoidance of evil" (Qur'ān 35:24; 25:51; 16:36); We sent no messenger but with the revelation that there is no God but God (Qur'ān 21:25). Thus, all excuses fall down. No matter how humans may have denied their humanity by refusing to perceive the truth of God, of His transcendence and unity, they were duly informed and warned by a messenger whom God had sent to them to teach them that truth in their own tongue and idiom (Qur'ān 14:4).

In this respect, Islām recognizes all Jews and all Christians as creatures of God, whom God had blessed with reason and understanding, sufficient to enable them to know God in His transcendence and unity; that being so endowed, they must have recognized God as God, one, transcendent and ultimate. Moreover, Islām acknowledges all Jews and Christians to have received from God messages through their prophet's teaching of the same lesson, so that if, *per impossibile*, they have missed what is natural and hence necessary to them, they were given it gratuitously as a gift from heaven, through prophecy. As such, the Jews and Christians are people with the true religion, the *dīn al fiṭrah*. No Muslim may deny this fact of nature without contradicting the Qur'ān and hence, abjuring Islām. Recognition of this truth is of his faith. Therefore, religiously speaking, the Muslim acknowledges the Jews and Christians to be endowed with the religion of God twice, once by nature and hence necessarily and universally, and once by the grace of God through their prophets.

B. The Level of the Semitic Tradition

Unlike the first level on which Islām regards the Jews and Christians as *de jure* possessors of true religion necessarily, i.e., by virtue of their birth as humans and their receipt of universal prophecy, this level regards them as possessors of true religion by virtue of their inheritance of the Semitic religious tradition. Religiously speaking, the Jews and

26

Christians are heirs of a genuine religious tradition, perhaps the greatest on account of its numerous prophets. History recognizes them as such. True, being the heir of a legacy is an accident of history, not a matter of necessity. The legacy of history may be denied or abandoned, and a new identity acquired. Belonging to one's legacy is a matter of choice. But the fact that Jews and Christians do belong to the legacy and regard it as their own is incontrovertible. Hence Islām acclaims them as partakers of the religion of God. True, they must accept the legacy and acknowledge it as a legacy of the religion of God. But those who do, Islām honors as possessors of true religion.

The Semitic legacy of religion, Islām holds, began with Noah. "God ordained for you the same religion He ordained for Noah," the Qur'ān affirms (42:13). "God chose Adam, Noah, the people of Abraham and 'Imrān... We have sent a revelation to you [Muḥammad] as We did to Noah and the prophets after him ... to 'Ād and Thamūd and countless others known only to God that came after them, and about whom We did not tell you, to them We sent Our prophets ... that there shall be no doubt in God, the Creator of heaven and earth... We have entered them all into Our mercy ... rehabilitated them and guided them to the straightforward path (Qur'ān 3:33; 4:163; 21:85; 6:86). Ancient history and archeology added to those whom the Qur'ān mentioned the names of Sargon of Akkad, of Lippit Ishtar, Hammurabi and others who promulgated laws which they received from heaven, and called all humans to abide by them in fidelity to God.

The religion of Noah's descendants consisted of principles which were repeatedly affirmed by all Semitic revelations. The first was the transcendence of God, affirmed in His ontological separateness from or otherness than His creation. The second was the relevance of God to His creation, constituting its *raison d'être*, its purpose and ought, the norms by which every creature is to live its life. The third is that this divine relevance is knowable to man, whether by divination (i.e., reading it in the omens of nature), science (i.e., discovering it in the inimitable patterns or laws of nature), or prophecy, the direct revelation of the will of God through words for the ready use of the understanding. The fourth is that humans are capable of fulfilling the divine imperatives, by virtue of the knowledge, actional capacity and subservience of nature to them, which God had endowed to them. The fifth and last is that humans are responsible and hence subject to judgment; to reward in case of compliance and punishment in case of defiance or violation. These five principles are the core and foundation of all Semitic religiosity, from Noah to Muḥammad. All those who belonged to the Semitic tradition acknowledged these principles regardless of whether they observed them or not in their everyday lives. And by doing likewise, the Jews and Christians establish their claim to the religion of

27

God. And to acknowledge this truth is integral to the faith of Islām.

C. The Particular Level of Judaism and Christianity

The foregoing acknowledgments of Islām, indubitable and unchallengeable to Muslims because they come as divine proclamations in the Qur'ān, were further reinforced by a third kind of justification: the direct kind. The first two levels effected their justification by laying down principles and declaring the Jews and Christians as instantiations of them. The third level confronted the Jews and Christians in their Judaism and Christianity head on, and declared them justified in the eye of God.

Those who believed—the Jews, the Christians, the Sabaeans, and others—who believe in God, the Day of Judgment and do the good works, stand to be rewarded by God. No fear or grief shall befall them (Qur'ān 2:62; 5:72). Say [to the Jews and Christians], we [Muslims] believe in that which was revealed to you. Our God and your God is One and the same. We all submit to Him (Qur'ān 29:46). Say, we [Muslims] believe in God, in what He revealed to us, to Ibrāhīm, Ismā'īl, Isḥāq, Ya'qūb and the tribes, to Mūsā (Moses), 'Īsā (Jesus) and all the revelations of the prophets—without discriminating between them. To God we submit (Qur'ān 2:136).

This constitutes more than justification of Judaism and Christianity. It is not only similarity, likeness or agreement of Judaism and Christianity with Islām. It is self-identification with them. Obviously no greater justification can be found or given. Islām regards the God of Judaism and Christianity as its own God, their prophets as its own prophets, their revelations and scriptures as its own revelation and scripture. Together, Islām holds the two religions and itself to be one religious fraternity. Nothing more could be asked or desired. Like the other levels of justification, this one too is Qur'ānic, held by all Muslims to proceed from God, *verbatim*.

This unity — nay, identity — of the three religions makes the Muslims regard the Jews and Christians as their brothers in faith in, and submission to, the one God of all. Disagreement between them there certainly is; but under the canopy of faith in God and belonging to His religion, all disagreements are domestic disputes. Indeed, there is no single criticism which Islām has addressed to either Judaism or Christianity or their adherents which Jews and Christians have not addressed to themselves or their tradition. The religious wish that Islām entertains regarding Judaism and Christianity is therefore the same wish entertained by countless Jews and Christians across the ages. Islām did criticize the Jews for failure to uphold the Torah (Qur'ān 5:71), for moral complacency (5:20), for excessive legalism and exaggerated authoritarianism by the rabbis (9:31; 3:50), for tampering with the texts

28

of revelation (4:45; 5:14). These are shortcomings which no honest historian of the Jews and Judaism can deny. Moreover, Islām never condemned the Jewish people *in toto*, since the critical verses stand side by side with those others which justify the Jews, both enjoying the same divine authority. And in order to dispel any such confusion, the Qur'ān explicitly distinguished the righteous from the unrighteous (Qur'ān 3: 113-114).

As to the Christians and Christianity, Islām criticized the deification of Jesus in no uncertain terms (Qur'ān 9:30), as well as the doctrine of trinitarianism (4:171-172), of monkery (57:27), and of exaggeration in matters of religion (4:171). But it has equally praised the Christians for their humility and altruism, their fear of God, and has declared them closest to the Muslims by their warm practice of neighborly love (5:82). True, Islām rejects the Christian claim that the texts of scripture are integral records of the message Jesus had conveyed. In this however, as well as in the other criticisms, Islām is not alone. Countless biblical scholars and theologians have said the same thing. Even among "the Apostolic Fathers," and certainly in the Nicene, anti- and post-Niceme Fathers, countless others have maintained more or less exactly what Islām did.

Now that I have stated how the religion of Islām regards Judaism, Christianity and their adherents, I wish to close with a statement of what we Muslims request of Jews and Christians. We have heard the distinguished speakers tell us what some Jews and Christians have said about Islām and the Muslims. It is disappointingly little. A religion's attitude toward Muslims who constitute almost a quarter of the human race cannot depend upon the opinion of a scholar or theologian whose authority is by nature limited. We salute and thank the Vatican for making a significant improvement of Catholicism's attitude to Islām and Muslims through Vatican II. Although it falls short of justification, the change is an admirable first step. Nothing has yet come from an authoritative Protestant body such as the World Council of Churches, the National Council of Churches around the world, from the Greek and Russian Orthodoxy, or any Sanhedrin or Rabbinic court. God's call to Jews and Christians still stands, as *à propos* and necessary today as it did when it was first revealed: "O People of the Book! Let us now come together under a fair principle common to all of us — that we worship none but God, that we associate nothing with Him, and that we take not one another as lords beside God" (Qur'ān 3:64). And nothing less than Islām's position will do, namely, the acknowledgement of Islām as a religiously legitimate religion by Judaism and Christianity. Until such acknowledgement is made, Muslims will stand far ahead of their Jewish and Christian colleagues in dialogue, goodwill and cooperation.

Topic II
THE NATION STATE AS FORM OF SOCIAL ORGANIZATION
CHAPTER 5
THE NATION STATE AND SOCIAL ORDER IN THE PERSPECTIVE OF JUDAISM

Seymour Siegel
Ralph Simon Professor of Ethics and Theology
The Jewish Theological Seminary of America

In the White House ceremony marking the signing of the Camp David Accords, President Jimmy Carter, a Christian, Anwar Sadat, a Muslim and Menachem Begin, a Jew — all quoted the same verse. They all alluded to the immortal words of the Hebrew prophets who foresaw a time when men shall beat their swords into ploughshares and their spears into pruning hooks.[1]

The vision of universal brotherhood and international peace so eloquently spoken by the prophets is part of the heritage of all the great religions of monotheism. Those who profess belief in the universal Fatherhood of One God also affirm the brotherhood of all men. Disharmony, hatred, and war cannot be in harmony with the will of the Father of us all.

The Judaic tradition has profound words to speak to our situation especially in the light of the subject we are discussing.

There are a series of antinomies which undergird the view of Judaism regarding the role of nations and the prospects for their unity.

The first antinomy realizes that though Man is universal, men are particular.

All men are created in the image of God. They all share in the same patrimony. Yet the one-ness of man is not the only testimony to the power and majesty of God. It is also man's particularity that procliams God's grandeur.

The talmudic rabbis, reflecting their awe in the presence of the Creator said:

---

1. Isaiah 2:4. The vision refers to *acharit hayamim*, the end of days. This is therefore an eschatological vision.

A man of flesh and blood produces many coins from the same die. They are all identical. But the King of Kings (that is God) stamps out all men in the die of Adam the first man. Yet not one man is identical with his fellow man.[2]

The identical origin of human beings in the Divine elevates the grandeur of human unity — yet the diversities of man testify to God's wisdom.

This does not only refer to the infinite variety of human talent and experience. It also posits the existence of a diversity of peoples. "When we see a soul we always see a community rising behind it"(J. Pedersen). In the Israelite conception no human being can exist except as a member of an 'am, a people. The belonging to a community, especially of those who share family ties and ancestral heritage is a prerequisite for *shalom* the greatest of all blessings. The word shalom means totality; it means the untrammeled free growth of the soul. "The soul can only expand in conjunction with other souls."[3]

Apart from the family the totality which has the strongest hold is that of the people. It is a kinship which extends in time. Each people has its own world.

The existence of these indispensible particularistic elements in human life does provoke inevitable tensions. The most effective state of mutual life is that of *berith*, covenant.[4] A covenant is a mutual agreement in which two or more entities agree to share some aspects of common existence. They enter into a promise to respect boundaries and to work together when necessary. *Berith* means establishing partial community. It does not mean amalgamation.

Thus the first antinomy: man is particular and universal at the same time. The vision of a peaceful world is not a vision of a world of sameness of the loss of communal or national identity. The nations will live together in peace: they will not live together a gigantic mass. It is covenant, not assimilation that is the *desideratum*. "A man's feet must be firmly planted in his own country, but his eyes must survey the world" (George Santayana).

The second antinomy affirms that the creation of the nation-state is

---

2. Talmud. Mishna Sanhedrin 4:3. The context is a warning to witnesses, especially in capital cases to be truthful and accurate in their testimony. If they cause the death of any person they are responsible for the death of a unique being which will never be replicated.

3. The discussion by Pederson, J.: *Israel*, Vol. II, pp. 84ff is subtle and is the best explication of the physic meaning of shalom that I know.

4. Pedersen, op. cit. Gerhard Von Rad, *The Theology of the Old Testament*, Westminster Press, sees the idea of covenant as the central concept of biblical religion. The same is true of Walter Eichrodt, *The Theology of the O.T.*

an outcome of evil. Yet there can be no significant life without some form of political organization.

If men were not sinful, there would be no need for the nation state. Men would live together in harmony, obeying the law of God and respecting boundaries and the rights of others. In the ideal situation, as Buber has pointed out[5] God is the King, and there is no need for earthly rulers. But men are sinful and therefore the coercive power of the government is a necessity.

In Biblical theology, the story told in the first book of Samuel about the beginning of the Israelite kingship is reflective of the polar evaluation of political authority.

The people had been ruled by the judges and prophets. They had no permanent political structure. The elders come to the prophet Samuel and say: "appoint for us a king to govern us like all the nations. (Samuel 8:5). Samuel sees this as a rebellion against God's rule. He is told indeed by God "Hearken to the voice of the people in all that they say to you; for they have not rejected you, but they have rejected me from being king over them," (ibid, 6:7). Samuel acquiesces and warns the people that the imposition of structured political authority will cost them dear in the surrender of their freedom to the sovereign. They continued to insist on the appointment of the king, despite the negative outcome. The appointment of the king is necessary to protect the people from the Philistine invaders.

In this incident, the political philosophy of the nation-state is enunciated. The state is indispensible, otherwise the threat of internal chaos and defenseless resistance to aggression will overwhelm the people. However, the necessity of the nation state does put into power groups of people over other people. The wielders of power face the constant temptation of increasing their power at the expense of the people. Therefore, the nation-state is a defense against sin, but it is also the vehicle of sin. "Pray for the welfare of the government," advise the talmudic rabbis, "for were it not for the fear of the government people would swallow each other up alive."

In the working-out of this paradoxical situation of the nation-state, the religous spokesmen have a role which is also fraught with ambiguity. It is the role of the religious institutions to undergird the common foundation which is the basis of the commonwealth. They are the guardians of the historical myths which enrich the culture of the community. They enunciate the "truths which are held self-evident," which guide the common life. The priestly function of the religion is

---

5. Buber's book, the *Kingdom of God*, is the best summary of the political outlook of the Hebrew scriptures.

vital to the health of the community. Yet, it is also the role — or perhaps chiefly the role — of the spokemen of the Deity to warn against the inevitable pretensions of the political leaders to illegitimately enlarge their power and to exploit their people. It is also the prophet who warns against cruelty to other nations. It is the task of the prophet to call to task the political leader who identifies his (that is the political leader's) interests with universal interests. The greatest danger emerges when the political framework becomes totalitarian making total claims on the loyalty of the people. The political realm has claims upon us, for its continued authority makes life tolerable. It cannot make claims of universal rectitude and absolute truth — for the state is only a concession to human sinfulness. This leads to the paradoxical assertion that a "secular" state whose laws and policies are provisional, open to compromise and change is more "religious" than a "religious" state. In a political system where the governmental policies are seen as the result of divine imperatives, there is no room for adjustment of policies to new realities. It is also an open invitation to tyranny and suppression of opposition — for the dissidents in this situation go not only against man, but against God. The prophets of Israel who criticize the king mercilessly represent the critique of religion of the pretensions of political power.

Therefore, the second antinomy of Judaic political philosophy recognizes not only the indispensibility of the nation-state, but also its dangers. It is true to its task when it continually reminds those who wield power — whether it be political, economic or even 'religious' — that there is a limit to their rights of sovereignty over their fellow man. It is only God Who can demand complete loyalty. All human institutions have a right to provisional authority — but become extremely dangerous when they identify their own policies with universal good.

The third antinomy can be stated in this way: the brotherhood of all men is a grand and profound dream — but its premature implementation can be destructive of man.

The vision of brotherhood and unity of all people fires the imagination and inspires the soul. It has been the aim of saints and politicians from the time of Alexander the Great. However, efforts to affect this dream can be destructive. That is because the ubiquitous tendency of men is to convert their own self-interest into a perceived universal interest. Therefore, attempts at unity which do not take account of the self-pretensions of those in power — or rather especially of those in power — can come to grief. The unity sought becomes a unity which crushes opposition and increases human misery. The *pax romana* in ancient times and the attempts of medieval Christendom in the middle ages are examples of the pernicious ways in which a great end becomes perverted by self-pretensions. The other side of the coin is the naive belief that goodwill alone will curb the appetite of others to swallow up their neighbors. Utopians of all stripes have to be reminded that the creation of a perfect society is not possible under conditions of historical time. Therefore, it is necessary to take precautions against aggression and the self-aggrandizement of neighbors. The balance of power (and terror) seems tragically to be the best guarantee of peace and harmony. Of course, there are breakthroughs. These are in the nature of covenants that are arrived at out of mutual self-interest or genuine morality. But even these arrangements are not absolute. They can deteriorate and radically change. Again we are at a paradox. We can best preserve peace — by being ready for war.

The marvelous exposition of the story of the Tower of Babel found in the book of Genesis by Reinhold Niebuhr sharply and clearly illustrates the antinomy and tragedy of good intentions frequently resulting in tragedy.

Niebuhr points out[6] that man's spirit drives him to seek eternal and universal goods. "He is not content to be merely American man, or Chinese man. He wants to be man." He therefore, tries to build temples of the spirit or of the government which will over-arch particularities. This is a necessary human enterprise. However, sadly, these towers of the spirit which seek so piously to see above the limitations of finite man inevitably become Towers of Babel which "pretend to reach higher than their real height; and claim a finality which they cannot possess." A striking example of the validity of Niebuhr's insights is the corruption and the achievements of the United Nations. That organization which sought to express the universal aspirations of mankind and to bring peace to a warring world has certainly some significant achievements to its credit. However, it is clear that the United Nations at the moment at least represents the interests of the dominant powers or the numerical majority. It does not represent universal man. As a matter of fact, it becomes dangerous when it pretends to do so. One can imagine what misery would ensue if the United Nations indeed had more power than it now has. The Tower is high. It pretends to reach to the sky, that is, higher than it really is. The result is confusion, strife, and evil.

The nations should strive to achieve partial unity. These are represented in what we have called "covenants". However in an unredeemed world, these are only partial achievements — not to be either underestimated or overestimated. Utopianism, which is idealism without realism, is both inevitably disappointing and in the end

---

6. The story of the construction of the Tower of Babel is found in Genesis, 11. It is apparently a story explaining the existence of some great ziggurat in Babylonia. Reinhold Niebuhr's essay on the story is found in *Beyond Tragedy*.

destructive, even if some partial good has been achieved.

Therefore, the antinomy is expressed. Man must dream the dream of a universal harmony. This dream should drive him toward improvement of the anarchic state in which we now find ourselves. However, biblical religion reminds him that in the complexities and ambiguities of contemporary history, there must be both a profound sense of responsibility to further the cause of brotherhood and a universal intelligence to recognize our limitations.

This leads to the final antinomy. In Judaic faith, the unity of man will be only in the end-time, when the evil inclination will be slain and human nature regenerated. That time is in the future in the *acharait hayamim*, in the end of history. But it is always with us. Every moment, as Buber said, must have a drop of messianism in it. The swords will be beaten into ploughshares from time to time but in historical time, not all swords can be turned into useful implements. What we must avoid at all costs are the twin dangers of utopianism which believes that the consummation of history can be achieved through human effort alone. This promises too much. The other danger is cynicism which posits that nothing can be done to improve and ameliorate human evils. The religous traditions provide the vision of human brotherhood. They should encourage efforts to bring the desired end closer. From time to time we have a taste of what human life can be. However, in Judaic thought at least, we are denied its full realization until the coming of the Messiah.

One idea is paramount in Jewish self-consciousness. That is the idea of exile. The world is in exile. In Jewish mysticism even God is in exile.[7] Yet, though in exile we remember the promise and try within our limitations to achieve that which we can achieve.

In sum, the religious traditions which we represent here can serve useful, though limited, purposes in overcoming the evils of nationalism and promoting international cooperation and brotherhood.

First of all, to persist in demanding that the dream be part of our action. That is the duty to deny the present situation ultimately. The religious should be aliens with uneasy feet. Not satisfied with any level of achievement. They should push for more and more cooperation.

Secondly, they should constantly remind those in power that

---

7. This startling idea is expressed in the kabalistic writers. The most subtle and interesting exposition of this view is found in the various writings of Professor Gershom Scholem, chiefly, *Major Trends in Jewish Mysticism*, Schocken, and *The Messianic Idea in Judaism*, Schocken. Valuable insights regarding the issue we are discussing will be found in Robert Gordis, *The Root and the Branch*, The University of Chicago Press, especially Chapter 11: "Nationalism and World Community."

whatever the divisions of mankind — and they are, as I have said, legitimate — there is an over-arching unity of mankind rooted in the fatherhood of God. This means though there are inevitable conflicts between peoples and nations, even our enemies are endowed God's image. They should be respected even in our self-defense against their attacks. This should lead to redoubled efforts to overcome differences and contract covenants.

Religious groups should help resist efforts at levelling of all men and should encourage the particularistic as well as the universalistic dimensions of human life. This group distinctiveness which is a necessary quality for the full realization of our selfhood frequently requires that groups achieve national sovereignty so as not to be overwhelmed by majorities or hostile neighbors. The only real basis for the preservation of separate national sovereignties is that they are necessary to the preservation of the soul of the people. They are also indispensible when there are competing sovereignties who seek the destruction and weakening of the people. Religions have frequently been irrelevant because they lacked *realism*. No ethic is useful if it fails to recognize the factors operating in the situation to which the faith-communities address themselves. We are trying to make the real world better — not some imaginary or ideal place. In the real world there is hostility, aggression, and bogus attempts at universalism which seek to undermine groups which are small and relatively powerless. Arrangements are necessary which will minimize harm but achieve a modicum of justice and assurance for all those who wish to live productive lives.

Religion should remind us that we are men and not gods; that we are limited in our achievements — though unlimited in our pretensions. We are bound by our limitations — but not paralyzed by them. In this situation there are enterprises of the human spirit which serve to help people transcend their national limitations and to associate with others who are of different allegiances. The work of science, of scholarship, of protection against the fouling of the atmosphere — these are some activities of men in which they unite not as Russians or Americans — but as members of the human race. The more such contacts are established, the more likely it is that nationalism will be less of a barrier to the achievement of human brotherhood. When men can establish covenants to make music or to fly to the moon — they will also be more likely to promote covenants which will to a modicum, at least, bridge over the barriers of nation, nationality, and race — to establish relationships which though not diminishing the distinctiveness of historical groups which are part of our world — will bring about friendship and cooperation — a relationship symbolized by the word covenant or *berith*.

These observations about the role of religion apply especially to the monotheistic religions — Judaism, Christianity, and Islam. They all worship the same God; revere the same historical personalities; and claim the same revelation. These groups should take the lead in promoting the brotherhood of man which is still to be realized.

Some will be disappointed that we cannot hold out the promise of the overcoming of all of the agonies of men in our world. It is the grandeur of our faiths that we are called to try to conquer evils one by one — and rely on the One to finally conquer evil.

CHAPTER 6
THE NATION STATE AND SOCIAL ORDER:
IN THE PERSPECTIVE OF CHRISTIANITY

John C. Raines
Associate Professor of Religion
Temple University

Christian history has developed two major traditions of reflection upon the nation state and the quest for political order. The first is the Augustinian tradition, which has had major influence upon such diverse groups as the pro-papal publicists of the 12th and 13th centuries and, far different, Martin Luther, John Calvin, and their modern interpreters like Reinhold Niebuhr.

The other tradition stretches back to Thomas Aquinas, and behind him to Aristotle and the classical idea of the *polis* as a *res ·publica*. Thomas influenced Roman Catholic thought upon the state from his own day down to the present. Especially is this the case if one interprets Aquinas as moving in the same direction as John of Paris and Marsilius of Padua in seeking to establish a purely *natural basis* for the state, independent of God's special revelation in Christ.

I plan here to analyze some of the principle ideas in each of these two traditions, ideas which are by no means always in agreement, and then apply this to our modern situation and its critical search for a stable world order.

I. Augustine:

For Augustine, the state is at the same moment an instrument of order and instrument of chaos. He did not believe this ambiguity could be transcended.

The state is, in its origin and essence, "a punishment for sin and a partial remediation of sin's worst affects" — (a *proenia et remedium peccati*). Why such a limited and morally suspicious view of the political order? For Augustine, the human person is not fundamentally rational. Reasoning, to be sure, is our species' peculiar property. But reason, so Augustine held, is not in itself the governing instrumentality of personal life. Rather the human is primarily a passionate being, a being of will — or, more simply, a creature driven by love *(dilectio)*.

For Augustine, reason does not transcend the special love the self has for its own interests. Rather reason *projects* those self-interests as of "universal" claim. The self is not so often made more impartial by its reasoning as its reasoning starts to parade its partiality as of universal merit. It is will and love that rule. And for fallen humanity (the vast majority), Augustine held that the love which rules cannot be anything else than that "disorderly love" *(dilectio inordinata)* which seeks to advance the self at the expense of all else.

What a person loves, that is what defines their personality and renders their activity coherent — even if that coherence is only one of wrongly placed love. Similarly, a collectivity of humans — be it tribe or nation or empire — is rendered understandable when one understands what love it is that unites them. Augustine looked upon the Roman Empire as an example of the general form or type of the state. To understand Rome, Augustine concluded, meant to understand Rome's common "love of glory" (their *libido dominandum*). It is this "love to dominate" that bound Romans together, and gave them a kind of common life.

Internally, Rome's common love of glory brought a relative social peace. It ordered the war of lesser loves — money, family, sex, etc. — into a common set of admirations. Admiring in common the acquisition of public recognition and command, the Romans had a kind of common or public life. It was a kind of domestic peace — the peace of the victors over the vanquished, cemented by the envy which the vanquished held for the victors, together with their desire to be like their overlords and not like themselves.

But this internal, domestic peace was extracted only at a terrible price — the price of international anarchy. Rome's common pursuit of glory secured internally an ordering of the war of lesser loves — providing a relative order of everyday sacrifice and duty. But it did this only by producing the international system as a system of perpetual instability and war. The only peace available *between* nations, Augustine held, is what he called "the peace of the graveyard" where, for a while, the winners preside over a kind of silence.

Moreover, the relationship between nations inevitably lacks that semblance of order which hierarchy and authority can secure within a nation. For there is between states no common agreement as to their lives, no common arbiter over their system of admirations, and so no agreement as to those who are to be admired and regarded as authoritative. Hannibal and Caesar were leaders of respective communities of shared admiration, but there was no higher dedication which could unite them. War remained their final court of appeal.

Worse yet, even amongst those who share a common religion, as the struggle between Christian Rome and Christian North Africa showed, there is no easy approach to common international agreements. Even religion does not automatically transcend the self's love of itself and its own. Sadly, religion is more often but an expression and servant of that love. Neither natural reason nor natural religion can extract man from sin — what Hobbes was later to call "the war of each against all."

Augustine begins his famous *City of God* by reflecting upon "these shifting sands where empires rise and fall," where "today's victor becomes tomorrow's vanquished," and where in the end "the dead make room for the dying." There is this deep strain of pessimism in Augustine. And it makes for a stark picture of limits to the moral expectations we can reasonably hold for international life.

All this was built upon Augustine's view of the human person. The self, for Augustine, is a *mediate being.* It stands midway between the fullness of being which is God, and that lesser thing which is the material world. Driven by its love, its search for happiness, the self seeks its satisfactions in that which is inherently fleeting — in the material, finite world. The self, which transcends its every immediateness with the world, and which cannot unite and exhaust itself with that which has less reality than itself — namely material goods however otherwise worthy — this self, I say, restlessly seeks its good — running first to this material satisfaction, and then to that. Driven by the insatiability of its need for significance, the self pursues a practical polytheism, making gods out of the many goods of the material world. Or it may practice a henotheism — ordering many goods under one good — like glory — which is itself, however, still finite. The self is thus either hopelessly diverse or prematurely closed.

This lack of internal integrity can be brought into order and tranquility only when unified by the love of God. "Our hearts are restless," Augustine says, "until they find their rest in Thee."

History, then, is composed of the history of two loves, and of the two cities formed by these two loves — one which "loves the self to the contempt of God" and the other which "loves God to the contempt of self." One is the city of this earth. The other is the city of God, or the Church — the earthly, but even more the heavenly community of saints. True, the heavenly city is "to make its peace bear upon the peace of this world." But Augustine expected little to come of such efforts. The history of nation states, their rise and their fall, remained for Augustine largely a backdrop of absurdity to that only meaningful passage of time which is the pilgrimage of the lost soul finding its way back home to heaven.

Here are Augustine's words as he laments upon the human condition. "Remember the rivers of Babylon," he says. "What are the rivers of

Babylon? The rivers of Babylon are all things which are here loved, and pass away. For example, one man loves to practice farming, to grow rich by it, to employ his mind on it, to get his pleasure from it. Let him observe the issue and see that what he has loved is not a foundation of Jerusalem, but a river of Babylon. Another says, it is a grand thing to be a soldier; all farmers fear those who are soldiers, are subservient to them, tremble at them. If I am a farmer, I shall fear soldiers; if I am a soldier, farmers will fear me. Madman! thou has cast thyself headlong into another river of Babylon, and that still more turbulent and sweeping. Thou wishest to be feared by thy inferior; fear Him Who is greater than thou. He who fears thee may on a sudden become greater than thou, but He Whom thou oughtest to fear will never become less.

"To be a lawyer, says another, is a grand thing; eloquence is most powerful; always to have clients hanging on the lips of their eloquent solicitor, and from his words looking for loss or gain, death or life, ruin or security. Thou knowest not whither thou has cast thyself. This too is another river of Babylon, and its roaring sound is the din of the waters dashing against the rocks. Mark that it flows, that it glides on; beware, for it carries things away with it.

"To sail the seas, says another, and to trade is a grand thing — to know many lands, to make gains from every quarter, never to be answerable to any powerful man in thy country, to be always traveling, and to feed thy mind with the diversity of the nations and the business met with, and to return enriched by the increase of thy gains. this too is a river of Babylon. When will the gains stop? The richer thou art, the more fearful wilt thou be. Once shipwrecked, thou wilt come forth stripped of all, and rightly will bewail thy fate in the rivers of Babylon, because thou wouldest not sit down and weep *upon* the rivers of Babylon.

"But there are other citizens of the holy Jerusalem, understanding their captivity, who mark how human wishes and the diverse lusts of men, hurry and drag them hither and thither, and drive them into the sea. They see this, and do not throw themselves into the rivers of Babylon, but sit down upon the rivers of Babylon and upon the rivers of Babylon weep, either for those who are being carried away by them, or for themselves whose wayward desires have placed them in Babylon?"

Here is that deep note of pessimism which lies behind what has come to be called Augustine's "political realism". It provides one mainstream in Christian thought about the state. It is a sober and sobering sense of limits, which works towards a quiet and unflashy political responsibility, of fanatical hopes. It is a realism which knows how many millions have been killed in the name of justice and honor. And it knows that those who did the killing always thought they were in the right.

What do we learn when we contemplate the nation state and the search for world order? For Augustine, we learn to discipline our moral expectations, and to act only from within that discipline. We learn that the best and only instrument of peace is an uneasy balance of power, and that all such balances of power are unstable and ultimately fleeting. We learn that "here there is no abiding peace," or ever can be.

II. Aquinas:

This Augustinian sense of tragic limits is, however, only one of the mainstreams in Christian moral reflection upon the state. Another, quite different and far more optimistic, is St. Thomas Aquinas.

For Aquinas the political order is part of the created order of nature, not a result of the fall. To understand the human person is to understand our being as essentially rational. Moreover, to understand humans as reasoning-beings means also to understand them as member of a common or public discourse. It is by talking together, Thomas held, that we actualize our human potential for rationality. By talking together we enter a world of shared meanings, and so come to order and make sense out of our life.

For Aquinas the political order is that *fundamental teacher* which wins us out of our "idiocy" — which is to say, out of our idiocycratic aloneness. The state is a *res publica*; it provides us with "common things" by which and within which we transcend our immediacy and carry on the common concourse of life. As human beings we are reasoning beings, and as reasoning beings we are necessarily social beings.

The fall damaged but did not fundamentally destroy this underlying capacity to reason, which means to reason together. Thomas maintained this position by distinguishing (as Irenaeus had centuries before) between the image of God (the *imago Dei*) and the likeness of God (*similitudo Dei*) — as first Genesis puts it, "in the image and likeness of God created He them."

In the fall, Aquinas held, we lose the likeness of God (the so-called theological virtues) but not the image of God — which is our natural rational capacity, and includes the first principles of morality. Far more than Augustine, Thomas stressed that it is reason that stands at the core of human personality. And reason is social; it is actualized only in *the talking of it*. Without this rational core, there can be no shared human perception of things, no common valuings and, consequently, no continuing order or coherence within which the will can take hold, have an intention, and follow through from means to ends. In sharp distinction from Augustine, from Thomas' perspective *selfishness presupposes society, and society presupposes a political order.*

"It is natural for man," Aquinas says, "to be a political and social animal, even more so than all other animals, as the very needs of nature indicate. For all other animals nature has prepared food, hair for covering, teeth, horns, claws as means of defense, or at least speed of flight. Man, on the other hand, was created without any natural provision for these things. But, instead of them all, he was endowed with reason, by the use of which he could procure all these things for himself by the work of his hands. But one man alone is not able to procure them for himself; for one man could not sufficiently provide for life, unassisted. It is, therefore, natural that man should live in the company with his fellows." (*De Reg. Prin. I.i.*)

Self-interest, for Aquinas, if perceived accurately, carries us not to individual selfishness but to "the common good". Public order is what we have in common; and it is what we have in common that blesses us.

This is Aquinas' positive doctrine of the state. Now what of his hopes for an international order? At least amongst Christian princes, his hopes were considerable.

The civil law (*jus civile*) of particular nations must hold itself accountable to the natural law (*jus naturale*) or "first principles of morality" which are available to all people through rational reflection. But what is to be done where Christian nations and rulers disagree as to the reasonable consequences upon their practical activity of this higher natural law? There must be an authoritative interpreter, one who normally does not interfere directly in the affairs of state, but who, upon extraordinary occasions, can and indeed must take a direct hand to arbitrate authoritatively conflicting claims for justice.

For Aquinas too, the rational agreement which can be secured amongst humans — especially humans of diverse customs and political communities — is fragmentary and precarious. It needs the firmer cement of authority. Thomas was hopeful about the prospects for order amongst Christian princes precisely because Christians, he thought, had such a higher authority in the head of the Church, the Pope of Rome. As Thomas said: "In order that spiritual matters might be kept separate from temporal ones, the ministry of this kingdom was entrusted not to earthly kings, but to priests and especially to the highest of them, the successor of St. Peter, vicar of Christ, the Roman Pontiff, to whom all kings must be subject, just as they are subject to Our Lord Jesus. For, those to whom the care of an intermediate end pertains should be subject to him to whom the care of the ultimate end belongs, and be directed by his rule." For St. Thomas, the end and goal of human life is heavenly blessedness. And that determines the final relationship between religious and secular authority.

The peace of the city of this earth — the maintenance of world order — depends for Aquinas upon the *mutually recognized authority* of the head of the Church at Rome. But already when Thomas offered this vision of hope, the events of history were carrying the Christian West

44

beyond any possible implementation of his hopes. The immediate future was to belong not to some unified Christian Empire but to individual nation states, where Christians would come to identify themselves first an Englishmen or Frenchmen or Germans, and turn in their hopes for peace not to the Pope but to the might of their national armies, or, later, to secular international organizations. The result is that peace has remained elusive and temporary.

III. The Situation Today:

What is the contemporary usefulness of this heritage of Christian reflection upon the state? I think both Augustine and Aquinas have something important to teach us. At the same moment, I also think the realities of our modern world now require a radical transformation of this heritage. First, the continuing usefulness ...

The hopefulness of Aquinas, his sense of the ultimate unity of all rational beings, can guard us against a premature despair about the prospects for our modern world. There is a terrible danger in the pessimism of Augustine when taken by itself. And it is a special danger to the affluent and comfortable. Put simply, it is much easier to contemplate the tragic moral limits of life when one is sitting beside one's suburban swimming pool than when one is walking the hot streets of the ghetto.

Hope deprivatizes our lives. It gives others a way of getting hold of us. Hope disciplines our private lives to hear and respond to the demand for justice by the oppressed. Augustine's sober realism needs the discipline of the hope of St. Thomas, and the trust he had in the fundamental rationality and social creativity of our species.

But it is also true — or it seems true to me — that hope needs the firm guidance of a sense of reality about the continuing selfishness of men and of nations. Otherwise hope cannot take hold in the world as it is. And when hope cannot take hold, it can become desperate, and can even be transmuted into a kind of anger and bitterness against humanity that it should remain so recalcitrant. Realism about self-interest guides hope into the paths of the possible, and keeps it from becoming a mere enthusiasm or, in its collapse, a prelude to cynicism.

This heritage of Augustine and Aquinas, then, has something important to say to us today. But at the same moment, at least to my mind, it is also true that the realities of today's world call for a radical transformation of this heritage.

Why? Because reality has changed. Old realisms have become far less real. Past Secretary of Defense Robert McNamara saw this. Reflecting upon the nuclear standoff between the super powers, he said: "Today we can no longer defend the people, we can only take revenge." Whether we speak of arms or of energy or of the economic transactions of multinational corporations, everywhere we see the realities of modern world spilling beyond national boundaries. Increasingly we live in a transnational world. But although we live transnationally we have not evolved effective instruments of transnational rule. International arms trafficking, for example, is out of the control of any one nation. Similarly, no single government — not even one as powerful as the United States — can bring the multinational corporation under effective public scrutiny and control. Or again, even the most powerful nations can no longer determine, by themselves, the patterns of their own energy use.

Nevertheless, people still think of themselves as members of nation states, not as citizens of the world. They identify themselves, which is to say they define their hopes and loyalties, as Americans or Russians or Egyptians. This puts us all in a most perilous position, because when we feel the inevitable pressure of our new transnational realities, our sympathies remain too parochial to do anything but resent that pressure. So we accuse our national leaders of "lacking leadership", when the truth is that no nation alone can lead the way it used to.

Even when people belong to transnational communities of religious faith, still their sympathies usually remain fundamentally defined by their national membership. In our Protestant Christian community, for example, we have evolved a World Council of Churches. It was established in 1948, two years after the United Nations. Today, these two bodies both suffer from the same internal tension. Both institutions were set up by the advanced industrial nations. Both institutions remain heavily dependent financially upon the richer nations. But by the 1970's both the World Council of Churches and the United Nations became composed of a majority representing the poorer and less developed nations.

This was inevitable. It simply reflects the realities of our world, where a few have very much in terms of affluence and power and the majority has very little. The result is that both institutions are now having difficulty with precisely those national communities which were so instrumental in their establishment. The danger is that the world's affluent and powerful will try to retreat behind their national borders. The danger is they will not see that their power is not so simply "their's" as it once was, that power is more and more transnational, that it is the power to cooperate and persuade.

All this puts world religions in a most unique and unprecedented position. Only the combined efforts of the world's great religions, I think, can break open our too narrow identities and too narrow sympathies. The old realism of "national interest" may still define reality for national policy makers. But within the world religions I sense a new realism growing. It is a realism that responds to a new sense of

46

how our species inhabits our precarious planet. It is the realism that we live in a world at once inextricably plural and inextricably interdependent. It is a realism that knows that a world as interdependent as ours cannot long remain as unequal as ours. It is the realism that knows that issues of distributive justice can no longer be absorbed into a rapidly and indeterminately expanding world economy.

Put simply, we stand on the threshold of a new world. And it is a world that has not yet found a way to make itself work! It is a world which challenges our religious heritages more fundamentally than anything any of us have ever had to face before. It is within our partly shared, partly diverse religious heritages alone, I believe, that we can find the moral vision to invest this new world with a sense of common citizenship. It does not mean that we must all become alike. It does mean that we must all become more equal. It does not mean we must all find one common religion. It does mean that we must learn each others' religions as a way of learning to respect one another. It does not mean the end of differences between us. It does mean that these differences must now be negotiated within what we know are the borders of a small and precarious planet.

The world is new. And it is a world where the old realism of "I want mine, now, more!" is prescription not for individual survival but for collective extinction.

******

I conclude by speaking from within my own tradition. The task of Christian political thinking today is to use our heritage to think our way into this radically new world, which could not be anticipated, a world whose only present order is the order of a common fear, and that is the fear of a world gyrating out of control, far beyond national sovereignties, towards a common disaster. Moreover, as Christians doing political thinking, we must recognize that our starting point is one of relative affluence and power, which must increasingly be shared with others. At least as European and North American Christians, our task is to persuade our fellow countrymen to the tasks of a new realism, a new way of life that is brought under the discipline of a more equal world.

In that task, we can learn from St. Augustine that unless one begins with where people are, with their given perception of their own self-interest, then you will not be able to move them. And from Aquinas we can learn that it is not impractical to hope that people will be rational, that if shown the impact of new world realities upon their old, more narrow perceptions of self-interest they will respond reasonably and modify their claims.

From Augustine we can learn that pious hopes without the astute use of power cannot change the world. And from Aquinas we can learn that religion has that kind of power. The power to define reality has traditionally belonged to religion; and it is a power whose responsibility, especially in these times, should bear heavily upon us. It is the power to legitimate or de-legitimate political authority, because religion defines the world within which leaders are perceived as truly leading, or only wandering.

Let us make no mistake. Political leaders can respond to new world realities only as religions redefine that world, and thus redefine what acting responsibly within that world means. I cannot overstate how seriously I think we need to take ourselves. Religion has been granted by most people in the world the power to tell them what is real. It is an awesome and terrible responsibility. We in religion have the power to legitimate or to de-legitimate secular rule. And our concrete situation is that the old way of making the world work no longer works.

The French existentialist Albert Camus spoke eloquently of this. "Tomorrow," he said, "the world may burst into fragments. In that threat hanging over our heads there is a lesson of truth. As we face such a future, hierarchies, titles, honors are reduced to what they are in reality: a passing puff of smoke. And the only certainty left to us is that of naked suffering, common to all, intermingling its roots with those of a stubborn hope."

We need a new politics, a politics guided by a new sense of what the future of the nation state must be if there is to be a human future at all. The prophetic voice of the world's religions is, I think the last best hope of humanity. This must be a voice critically aware of its own parochial base, and so able to transcend its narrow self-interests towards a more comprehensive hope. This hope must be pursued within the tension of the Augustinian sense of the tragic limits of human moral achievements, and the optimism of St. Thomas about what may still be possible when the full dimensions of our predicament become clear.

CHAPTER 7
THE NATION-STATE AND SOCIAL ORDER IN THE PERSPECTIVE OF ISLĀM

Ismā'īl R. al Fārūqī
Professor of Islamics
Temple University

I. The Family: First Level of Social Organization.

Human association has had a long history which three institutions had struggled to dominate. The first is the family, which has blood and heredity for bases. The characteristics it engenders in humans are innate and immutable. Indeed, they are constitutive of the relationship. Certainly family-living engenders in humans other characteristics which are acquired through association. These, however, are not necessary. Members born to one family may successfully be brought up as members of another; but the innate characteristics remain unchanged. The family was declared by God an intrinsic order of creation. "O Humankind, revere your Lord Who created you of a single soul and created of it its spouse... It is of God's providing that He created of yourselves spouses in whom to find quiescence, and established between you love and compassion...that He generated from you and your spouses your children and grandchildren."[1] Parents, their children and grandchildren, and the love and compassion relation between them, constitute an immutable pattern of God in creation. This is the family in its nuclear and extended forms spanning three generations. Islām not only acknowledges it but has girded it with law. Unlike any other social system, the law of Islām articulated the relations of all members of the extended family in order to insure proper functioning of all of them. Marriage and divorce, legitimacy and dependency, earnings and support, inheritance, and the members' mutual rights and duties have been detailed by the *shari'ah*. Matters which are not dealt with by any law, hardly ever considered by custom,

---

[1] *Qur'ān 4:1; 16:72; 30:21.*

or spoken of in public (e.g., the sex relations between the spouses) — let alone the more common affairs of everyday living — have also been defined by Islāmic law in terms of rights and obligations. Justice and equity are as much involved here as in any other human transaction. Delinquency may be estabished with precision, and dealt with effectively. On top of all the laws stands the divine commandment that mutual love and compassion, kindness and gentleness, and what is usually normative (*al ma'rūf* — Qur'ān 2:180, 228, etc.) should govern all intra-family relations.

The extent of the extended family is three generations inclusive of all members. Although Islāmic law left open the possibility to include members of other generations as need and the particulars of the case dictate, it assumed that those are included who can effectively eat from one kitchen and live in one estate. It assumed that through their shared living, which is possible for three generations but extremely difficult for more, the feelings of love, compassions and *ma'rūf* proper to the relation could be effectively maintained. The extended family is therefore the area where immutable factors constitute the sufficient reason for human association and where promoting these factors and using them as criteria of desirability or ethicality is legitimate and indeed commendable. It is not ethically improper to love one's spouse, one's children, one's brothers and sisters, one's grandparents and grandchildren, one's uncles, aunts, nephews and nieces because they are relatives. To love them for their wisdom or piety or achievement is worthy, but additional. Indeed, it is not ethically improper to define a person in terms of his or her family relation. To build over this relation an effective association to promote their welfare, to the exclusion of all other humans, is ethically desirable.

II. The Tribe or Nation: Second Level of Social Organization

The second institution to dominate human association is the ethnic communtiy or unit; and its pursuit is ethnocentrism.

A. The Ethnocentric Claim

Ethnocentrism is the view that man is definable in terms of the ethnic entity to which he belongs; that the good of the ethnic entity is the ultimate criterion of good and evil; and that humans ought to be guided in their conduct on earth by ethnic realities and values as principles. The ethnic entity is the tribe or nation. Its existence is necessary and justifiable by virtue of the biological, geographic, psychic, historical and political facts on which it rests.

1. The Biological Base

The biological basis consists of qualities which physical anthropologists study — the color of the skin, the shape of facial and skull bones, the form of eyes, nose and mouth, bodily build, and other innate physical characteristics inseparable from the person. These, every human gets neither by decision nor achievement. They are simply given by God at brith. Whether they are of this or that variety is neither the work nor the decision of the creature, but of the Creator. It is He Who determines them for all humans. But they belong to the first level of social organization, *viz.*, the family. They are not true of all members of the tribe or nation, though they are necessarily true of the family. It is also possible to establish occurrence of them outside the family. However, the farther one moves from the family, the more diffuse these characteristics become and the less predictable. Only racists would claim such innate characteristics to belong necessarily to all members of the group — the tribe or nation — which they call "the race." But their claim is false.

2. The Geographical Base

Humans, it is affirmed, live not no-where, but somewhere, within a definable territory. The tribe/nation lives on a land endowed with its own topography, location, aridity or fertility, its flora and fauna, its mountains and forests, its rivers and deserts, its lakes and seas. Tribes or nations differ from one another territorially. Their lands are separated from each other by physical boundaries (rivers, mountains, seas) or by imaginary political lines created by man (barbed wire fences, walls, etc.).

True as this may be, human belonging to a territory is not necessary. Human history has known many massive migrations of peoples from one territory to another. Modern technology, transportation and communication are making it more and more possible for humans to change territories at will. There is no necessity to one's continuing to live in the village, city or province of one's birth. The fact that a person was born, or resides, in a given territory does not define him; nor does it determine his worth as a human. The enlandisement of man is a debasement of him; for it defines or evaluates the person in terms of an accident of birth or history; and commits the reductionist fallacy by doing so in terms of that which must needs be evaluated rather than provide the criterion of evaluation. Just as humans are not definable, and far less subject of evaluation, by what they eat or put on, they are no more so by the real estate they own or the street address they occupy. It is far more becoming to define humans by the highest principles they acknowledge and by which they order their lives — namely, by their ideology or religion.

3. The Psychological Base

The tribe/nation is equally claimed to rest on a common psyche shared by all the members. This consists of psychic qualities such as language and dialect, habits of mind and perception, taste and sense of beauty, customs and mores, sense of humor and levels of concern and responsiveness. These shared characteristics, it is claimed, constitute

51

"national character," a "national ego or psyche," distinguishing one tribe/nation from another and justifying its distinction from all others. The essence and value of a person are functions of his instantiation of national character, of his concretization of the national ego.

Language, dialect, and customs, as well as the senses of humor and beauty, may well be shared by members of a tribe/nation. Their sharing, however, is not innate, but acquired. It is the result of many years of acculturation and socialization, of formation by the group, which may succeed in making the person an instance of the homogeneous group, and may not succeed. "National character" therefore is not so much a reality as it is a generalization. It is a hypothesis based upon a percentage, a certain frequency of occurrence. It is not necessary. Moreover, it is not an intrinsic good, but an instrumental one, deriving its value from the deeds of morality to which it prepares the individual, if at all. It is neither universal nor necessary. Moreover, its presence 'proves no more than its instantiation in the person, leaving that person's moral worth or unworth utterly untouched. a perfect "specimen" of its embodiment may be compared to a bow ready for the arrow. But nobody mistakes the bow for the hunter, or confuses their different values.

4. The Historical Base

The experiences which befall humans accumulate, and confirm one another. Eventually, they build up a tradition. Tradition constitues a fiduciary framework which affects the members of a tribe/nation, and determines their perception of their past, present and future as well as their conduct. It generates in them a feeling of continuity with previous generations, of belonging to one another's contemporaries, and a capacity to bear events and forge a future continuous with the past. Tradition is essential for the tribe or nation and indeed, constitutive. It not only distinguishes the nations from one another, but indicates their individual and comparative worth. It may well then provide the criterion of worth and unworth for persons inasmuch as their belonging to this or that tradition makes them members of this or that tribe or nation and predetermines their conduct.

History, and the tradition it builds, are perhaps the most important elements justifying the tribe or nation. Certainly, history is one of the factors which cause the group to emerge as a separate entity by its disciplining, instructing and homogenizing effect. But it is not the only agent. Nor does it determine conduct with necessity. A critical view of one's history and tradition is not only possible, but necessary for any significant human advance. Otherwise, life becomes too repetitious to be interesting. Moreover, great revolutions would be inconceivable; and so would massive conversion to a new faith. Where history is the criterion, the present and future can be only a replica or *taqlīd*. Where history and tradition are material to be judged by the tribe's or nation's absolute and a priori principles, the present and future can become the occasion for its transformation into something different and worthier, new and greater. Even a total abnegation of history cannot be ruled out merely on the ground that it is history. For it may well be desirable — nay, ethically necessary — to turn one's back to history and turn a new page, as those who turned to Islām or Christianity did during the last twenty centuries, or those who turned their backs to the "old world" and sailed for the "new" did in the last four. In all these cases, far from justifying anything, history and its tradition were the materials crying for justification which they never obtained from within themselves.

5. The Political Base

Finally, it is claimed that a tribe/nation rests ultimately on the will of its people to be a tribe or nation, autonomous and separate from all others. Their identification of themselves as different and their desire to perpetuate and institutionalize this differentiation constitute the necessary accreditation. This general will is equally the source and base of sovereignty which is the power of the group to determine its present and future in accordance with the consensus of its members, and to impose such determination in case of absence of such consensus.

Like the psychological base, the general will and sovereignty are instruments, not ends. Their values are preparatory only, and hence derivative from those of the ends to which they lead and which they are manipulated to serve. By themselves, they do not justify anything, not even their own existence. For that can be as much a cause of ultimate good as of ultimate evil.

B. The Islamic Position

1. Descriptive vs. Normative

It follows from the foregoing that all the elements on which the tribe or nation is based are not necessary, though they may be universal. They could be otherwise than they are. To alter them is indeed possible, not only in childhood where alteration would be most effective and permanent; but also in adulthood where deliberate decision, resoluteness and perseverence could change them just as perfectly. A person's membership in the tribe or nation does entitle him to love, honor, assistance and protection by fellow tribesmen on the basis that charity begins at home or, as Islāmic jurisprudence has formulated it, "the nearer is more entitled to your good deed (al ma‘rūf) than the farther." But this principle is not abolute. It is limited by the nature of the content of the claim. By virtue of belonging to the tribe, for instance, the tribesman is no more entitled to one's charity than the distant neighbor whose need for that charity is greater; nor for one's protection if the distant nieghbor stands in greater need for that protection. However, the near neighbor is indeed entitled to a minimum-survival, safety of body and property, freedom from disease, and education. He is entitled to these necessities of existence with priority. But he is entitled to no more than these necessities until the distant neighbor has achieved same. In no case does the need of the near neighbor entitle him to pursue these necessities at the cost of any other human, near or distant. That would be theft. Colonialism is precisely that; *viz.*, to exploit coercively for the benefit of one's fellow tribesmen the resources of the distant neighbor, or other tribesmen. If done without coercion, it is trade which may bring advantage or disadvantage to one or both partners. But with coercion, it becomes criminal, worthy of forced restoration of the robbed wealth as well as grave punishment.

Being a realistic religion bent upon the promotion of human welfare, Islām did not deny that humans are born into their tribes and/or nations; or that they become socialized into them by historical accident. This much of the claim of the advocates of particularism or ethnocentrism is not denied. Had Islām denied it, it would have had to wage an impossible battle against the hundreds of ethnic groups it had penetrated, a war in which it or the other party would have had to be annihilated. In fact, Islām never waged such a war. It tolerated the existence of ethnic characteristics as God-given as long as they remained in place. Once they interfered with the purposes of the *sharī'ah*, then they were curbed by the very people they characterized, as those people developed the higher loyalty to Islām and its vision. Language is the most important element of ethnicity. Its relation to Islām is a true index of Islām's position toward ethnicity as a whole. It is a commonplace fact that the native languages of the Muslim World not only survived, but were developed and became richer through the advent of Islām. Indeed Islām lifted many of those languages from the primitive level, to that of ordered structure, literacy, and endowment with a great legacy of literature. The legacies which developed in Persian, Turkish, Urdu, Malay, Hausa, and Sawahili are of world significance as well as inconceivable without the influence of Islām.

2. The Positive Good of the Tribe or Nation

Human acculturation and socialization through the tribe or nation of one's birth was ordained by the Creator. However, the purpose of the wider association differs. "O Humankind," the Qur'ān affirms, "We have created you all of a single pair, and We have constituted you into tribes and nations that you may know one another. The nobler among you is the more righteous" (Qur'ān 49:13). The purpose of belonging to this or that tribe or nation is identification. That this man is English and that one is Japanese, that one is black and the other is white, that one speaks Persian and the other Arabic, that one resides in Moscow and the other in Chicago — all these are aids in identifying the person. They do not tell us anything about the person's worth as a human. That is why God explicitly added to His Qur'ānic declaration the conclusion that the criterion of comparative worth among humans is righteousness. This addition is meant to deny that belonging to this or that tribe or nation constitues any criterion of worth.

Under a variant interpretation, the world *lita'ārafū* (that you may know/identify one another) of the Qur'ānic verse quoted earlier may be taken to mean "that you may cooperate with one another in doing *al ma'rūf* or the good deed." In this case, ethnicity becomes a good which serves as a base for *al ma'rūf*. Undoubtedly, the development of an ethnic language and its endowment with a literary tradition is a *ma'rūf*, a commendable achievement. The same may be said of other elements of ethnicity: music, dress, food, architecture, village or urban planning, social custom.

All these positive aspects of ethnicity Islām acknowledges under the *"ummah,"* as theoretical category, and all their values are subsumed under the *"ummah"* as axiological category. This particular meaning of the *ummah* (the *ummah* in this or that region of the world) constrasts with the universal *ummah* which is the first object of the world-state of Islām. To each, Islām and its law have assigned its proper place. The nearest Western term which covers the regional *ummah* is patriotism. Patiotism is the love, compassion and responsibility one feels toward his neighbors, his fellow tribesmen, his region of the globe. Islām appreciates these feelings. Indeed, it provides laws for the actualization of these objectives. Service to tribe or nation, it holds, defence of the regional *ummah* when aggressed upon from within (gangsterism, rebellion, breakup of public order) or from without (invasion, subversion) are duties under Islāmic law. Their neglect or violation is punishable in this world and the next. Thus Islām outdoes Western patriotism by making the ethnic group's service and defence a civic as well as religious duty. Islām doubles the motivation for compliance with patriotic requirements, by adding the punishment and reward of the other world to those of this world.

3. Patriotism vs. Ethnocentrism/Nationalism

Patriotism however, is radically different from nationalism, or ethnocentrism. The latter go far beyond patriotism as we have defined it. First, nationalism or ethnocentrism assumes the existence of characteristics in the group which biology knows to exist only in the family among people related in blood through a very few generations. This is the blunder of racism, which asserts the presence of biological qualities in the group to justify the separatism of its members from, and their superiority over, humanity. The "master race" and the "chosen people" theories with which this century made us all too familiar, are

55

examples of biology-based racism, the one defining membership in terms of descendence from mother, the other in terms of descendence from mother and father as well as eyes and hair color and cephalic index.

Second, ethnocentrism/nationalism considers all acquired group characteristics as necessary as the innate family characteristics, and treats them as such. For it does not differentiate between the necessities of biology and history. Its vision is so committed to the group that it reads into group history an absolutely necessary march which could not have been but as it was and is. Through mythologization, it creates gods out of the group's past and prostrates itself in worship at their feet. The accidents of history are fused with biological qualities assumed to exist in the group to form a mystical block with which the group is identified and its destiny charted.

Thirdly, nationalism/ethnocentrism assigns to the hypostasized biological-historical characteristics of the group universal value. In its axiological hierarchy, the values of other groups find only inferior, secondary position. The very existence of other groups is assigned instrumental status and value in relation to those of the nationalist/ethnocentrist group. The nationalist good is the highest. It must be pursued *überhaupt*; i.e., it must be the ultimate end of all other pursuits, and as such, all other pursuits are to become subservient to it. This is the axiological foundation which justified in the eye of the nationalist/ethnocentrist, his violation of all other groups, which indeed regards such violation not only permissible where it is instrumental to the nationalist good, but even obligatory when the two run in opposite directions. The nationalist/ethnocentrist group is egotistic, preferring its own good to that of humanity.

Promotive as it is of patriotism, Islām has no countenance for nationalism/ethnocentrism. It condemns it for its falsity, its pretense, and its truncated, reductionist axiology. Islām regards it as violating the most basic intuitions and values of humanity, as well as the highest commandments of God. Indeed, Islām regards nationalism/ ethnocentrism as a threat to divine transcendence. For under nationalism/ethnocentrism, humans are not the equal creatures of God who compete for merit with Him. They are unequal creatures and their inequality is not a consequence of their effort, but a function of their creatureliness. Furthermore, as preferred or chosen creatures, possessing higher values in their beings (i.e., ontologically), they stand to God in different relation that other creatures do. A god that suffers himself to stand in such different relations to his human creatures is not the transcendent God of Islām, but a prejudiced weakling, dominated by an irrational, arbitrary passion for his preferred stock. No wonder that nationalism/ethnocentrism conceives of Him as "the God of

56

Promise," i.e., as straightjacketed by his own promise given to his chosen, to which he is bound regardless of the chosen's conduct. The God of Islām is indeed the "God of the Covenant." But the covenant of God is an open covenant which all humankind are invited to enter. It is a free, open, two-way highway in which man serves God in loyalty to Him and God disburses His rewards according to personal merit. Nationalism/ethnocentrism reduces the God of the covenant to the God of the Promise and thus ruins His transcendence.

4. Nationalism/Ethnocentrism in History

Nationalism/ethnocentrism dominated life in Arabia before Islām, and was called *aṣabīyat al jāhilīyah*. It raised the tribe above humanity, focussed all poetry and feeling upon the tribe's glory, and demanded exertion of all effort in pursuit of the tribe's welfare. In the process, it justified raiding of the other tribe, robbery of its wealth, and slaughter of its innocent members for no crime but the fact of their belonging to another tribe. In order to eradicate this evil, Islām abolished the tribe as form of human association, and built the *ummah* on trans-tribal, humanity-wide foundations. it was to an Arab audience that the Prophet Muḥammad (ṢAAS) addressed the following admonitions on his last pilgrimage to Makkah, and hence the holiest occasion: "Listen to me well, O People, God created you all descendants of Ādam He created of earth. No Arab has any priority over a non-Arab, no white over a black and no non-Arab over an Arab, or a black over a white—except in righteousness."

Later in Islāmic history (first century of the 'Abbāsī caliphate, from about 150/775), the same evil showed its head again, this time under the name *"shuʿūbīyah"* (factionalism). But the *ummah* combated it successfully and eradicated it.[2] In modern times, it has risen again among Muslims in the aftermath of colonialism under the name *"qawmīyah"* or nationalism. Fortunately, *qawmīyah* has not penetrated to the Muslim masses, who remain aware of but one identity – the Islāmic – from the Atlantic to the Pacific. *Qawmīyah* was adopted by a Westernized upper crust of Muslim society which had been trained by the colonialists to hold the reins of power after their departure and to perpetuate the fragmentation of the world-*ummah* into mutually conflicting factions. Like the *shuʿūbīyah* of early Muslim history, modern *qawmīyah* is devoid of thought, but it is far more dangerous. It seeks to attach itself to Islāmic civilzation to which it has yet contributed nothing. As *shuʿūbīyah* was the camouflage of *zandaqah* (pretense of Islām shown by non-Muslims), *qawmīyah* is the pretense of anti-Arab or anti-Islāmic forces in the Muslim world

[2]For a detailed account, see Aḥmad Amīn, *Ḍuḥā al Islām* (Cairo: Maktabat al Nahḍat al Miṣrīyah, 1956), Vol. I, pp. 57ff.

seeking the division of the *ummah* into ethnic/linguistic/ geographic units which Islām never recognized. *Qawmīyah* is the committed enemy of the universal brotherhood of Islām, of world-unity under the aegis of Islām. Undoubtedly, the opposition of *qawmīyah* to the world-*ummah* will be the "battle of the century."[3]

Nationalism/ethnocentrism is built upon a relativist axiology. The scale of values as well as the higher values in the hierarchy are regarded as normative only for the group. The others may be its objects, or instruments, never its ultimate purpose which must be the group itself. That is why the God of nationalism/ethnocentrism may reach humankind, not in love or compassion but in revenge and vindication for the ethnic group. Equally, just as ethnocentric religion is hardly ever missionary, seeking deliberately to contain itself within the group and absolving humankind from equal obligation under the commandments of God, nationalism seeks to shut itself from humanity by setting for itself a temple, or holy ground, out of a piece of real estate it cuts off from the earth, and girds itself against humankind by restrictive citizenship and immigration laws. Little does nationalism/ ethnocentrism know that any sub-group within the group has more title to separatism and exclusivism than the group itself of which it is a part. For the more restrictive and smaller the sub-group, the more accurate its description of itself, and the stronger the *'aṣabīyah* (cohesive bond) among its members. Little does nationalism/ethnocentrism realize that by its own logic, it dooms itself to infinite fragmentation into ever smaller sub-groups, a fate it escapes only by contradicting itself, by denying its own logic. But, founding itself upon feeling, it takes refuge in the arbitrary judgment of ineffable experience. Little does it realize how perilously close it stands to the dogmatism of the Catholic Church, opposition to which gave nationalism ethnocentrism its birth certificate.

The nation-state is a phenomenon of European history. It arose as an expression of nationalism/ethnocentrism. Its origins are to be found in the Reformation. Having abused the peoples under its care, the Roman Catholic Church became the object of resentment by many. Its justification of its tyranny and abuse by declaring its practices consistent with its ideal of the universal *oikumene* (community) make the ideal itself hateful along with the practices. Thus, rebellion against the Church of Rome was at once rebellion against "aliens" who exploited the people, extorted their wealth and spent it on the beautification of alien lands (Italy). Rallying around the prince and against the Church of Rome was "national liberation" from that yoke. Thus the nationalist movements of Europe began. Later, when seventeenth century

---

[1]For an account of its literature, see this author's *On Arabism* (Amsterdam: Djambatan, 1961), pp. 121ff.

58

rationalism and the Enlightenment, in their combat of the dogmatism of the Roman Catholic Church, projected against the old ideal of the universal community but as the necessary consequence of rationalism, the mind of Europe was revulsed. In its second rebellion against universalism (whether religious, rationalist or secular) Europe flung itself violently toward ethnocentrism. The new movement was known as romanticism. It developed an epistemology of feeling and experience on which to base its religion (Schleiermacher), and ethic (Fichte, Nietzsche); and it relegated rationalism and empiricism to the sciences of nature alone. Group self-assertion became the order of the day in Europe. Inter-group conflict was mitigated only by the rivalry of European nations to invade and colonize Africa, Asia, Oceania and Latin America. Even so, wars between the European nations never ceased with one ethnic group claiming superiority over its neighbors, its colonies and the whole world. The Muslim world received the brunt of Europe's colonialist expansion. The terrible mess in which the whole world finds itself today is the direct consequence of European nationalism/ethnocentrism. Indeed the world is groaning under its yoke, and looks to the day when it could be liberated from it. Its contagion however is spreading to the Third World, just as the colonialists had planned in the hope of keeping its peoples divided against themselves and hence weak and exploitable.

III.   The Universal Brotherhood Under the Law: The World-Ummah

The third institution to dominate human association is the universal community. It was first established in history in the Akkadian, and later in the Babylonian, state in Mesopotamia. Although these states never extended beyond the Tigris-Euphrates valley and/or geographic Syria, they were thought by their rulers and citizens to cover "the four directions of the world." Every Arab migration into Mesopotamia and/or the Fertile Crescent (Akkadian, Amorite, Aramean) tended to repudiate the city states in favor of one which included the whole region which was the extent of their knowledge of the world. The peoples of the most distant areas were regarded as *de jure* citizens of the Semitic universal state, as witness the code of Hammurabi; whereas the Egyptians, the Greeks and the Romans never looked upon the citizens of the distant lands except as strange aliens and subject people to be colonized.

The ideal of the universal community was equally taught by Jesus, son of Mary, as the antidote to Jewish ethnocentrism. The same teaching was promoted by his followers who took the new religion outside of the Jewish community and proselytized the world. The ideal remained active in the Roman Catholic Church for almost a millenium and a half; but its history has been made turbulent by two factors militating against it. The first was the commonplace human failure to live by the high ideal. The second, unique to Christianity, was her condemnation of all political life as fallen, necessarily sinful and hopelessly incapable of achieving true felicity and salvation.

Islām was the ideal's greatest affirmation; and the Islāmic state, its greatest embodiment. Islām offers the universal community as base of human association, instead of the nation, people or ethnic group. This is not the *ummah* of the Muslims, or Muslim community, which is only a segment of the constituency of the Islāmic state. In the first written constitution, which was given by the Prophet to the New Islāmic state in Madīnah, the *ummah* of Muslims was *one* community, and the *ummah* of Jews was another. Later, the *ummah*(s) of Christians, Zoroastrians, Hindus and Buddhists joined the Islāmic state. The Islāmic state itself was an *ummah* of a different order, an expanding world-*ummah* designed eventually to include humanity as its citizens. The communities which constitute the world-*ummah* were to co-exist in peace. Each *ummah* is to order the lives of its members according to its own religion. It is to have its own institutions and its own laws, as well as the power to activate the former and implement the latter. The Islāmic state guarantees these perogatives in its *sharī'ah*, or God-given law and constitution. Within the world-*ummah*, everyone should be free to convince and be convinced of the truth. The divine commandment, "No coercion in religion" (Qur'ān 2:256) is to govern the relations of Muslims and non-Muslims alike.

The world-*ummah* of Islām was a radical and new political ideal then, as it is today; for the need for it continues persistently. It is a pluralistic universal society in which all humans are members by virtue of their birth, and members of a religious *ummah* by virtue of their religious affiliation. Its pluralism is based not on courtesies or arrangements and treaties which can be denied or revoked at the whim of politicians, but on laws which no earthly authority can change or revoke. Moreover, it is not a pluralism in the matters which do not count, such as one finds today in London or New York. It is a pluralism of law — an idea of which the West has not yet even conceived. Beside the *sharī'ah*, whose laws govern the lives of Muslim citizens and are administered in Muslim courts, the Islāmic state has the Torahic, Christian, Zoroastrian, Hindu and Buddhist laws which govern the lives of their adherents and are administered by Rabbinic, Christian, Zoroastrian, Hindu and Buddhist courts. Where the jurisdiction of these courts overlaps, as when the cases presented to them involve adherents of many faiths, the courts reconcile their verdicts together for the good of the adherents and the world-*ummah* of which they are the constituents. Only in matters of war and peace affecting the world-*ummah* as a whole is the Islāmic state exclusively the judge.

The Islāmic state is hence a world-state, with an army on the ready to repel aggression as well as to prevent war between one *ummah* and another. It is a *pax islamica* in which a person is identified according to what he cherishes best, his religion, ideology and law, not his tribal membership. It is a United Nations with teeth, so as to preserve the peace, and with respect and concern for the spiritual identity of the members. It is the expression of Islāmic humanism.

The raison d'être of the ummah — with its government and institutions — is not merely to curb the evil tendencies of man. To restrict the origin and purpose of political organization to the task of protecting the individual from the *bellum omnium contra omnes*, the presupposition of liberal political thinking in the West, debases the state and truncates it. Even if true, such prejudgments against it reduce the state's value to that of a preliminary condition. Underlying this thinking is the doctrinal position of Christian dogma, namely, that man is fallen, essentially vitiated by "original sin", and hence hopelessly embroiled in a predicament from which he can never extricate himself. Such a view is the presupposition of Christian soteriology. It has no place in Islām where man is held to be innocent, created in the best of forms, higher than the angels, and commissioned *(mukallaf)* with a task of cosmic significance, namely, to do God's will on earth, to realize the absolute in this space and time. To this end, God has made the whole of creation subservient to man, and created him capable of free action. The causal system of creation which is sustained and ordered by God was broken open only for human action to intervene and effectively to change the course of events and transform creation into the pattern God has commanded and revealed. This is the meaning of man's *khilāfah*, or vicegerency of God; of his carrying the *amānah*, or divine trust in space-time.

Evidently, if man is to pursue this end and actualize it, he needs the state. Being an ethic of works rather than an ethic of faith or intention, the ethic of Islām requires and presupposes the ordered society. For only there will man be able to fulfill the commandments of God. These, being all social, or ummatic in character, society, its institutions and the whole web of societal relations in which man stands are necessary. The state is not merely a policeman; though it does fulfill this function when and where necessary. Rather, the state is the focus of ummatic activity. It is the leader and mover which mobilizes and organizes human energies; which leads the ordered energies of the ummah effectively toward the goal. That history has known some men bent upon mischief, some rulers who have fallen to corruption and tyranny, constitue no attack upon the state and no argument against its desirability and legitimacy. The onward march of humanity toward the *khilāfah*-goal is the only legitimate criterion of worth. It justifies the state and all its institutions. But it also lays the greatest burden of responsibility upon it — the responsibility of fulfilling or not fulfilling the divine imperative, as well as that of Ultimate Judgment where every person, ruler or ruled, will get exactly what he or she has earned, blest or unblest.

Topic III
THE FAITH COMMUNITY AS TRANSNATIONAL ACTOR FOR JUSTICE AND PEACE
CHAPTER 8
THE FAITH COMMUNITY AND WORLD ORDER: THE PERSPECTIVE OF JUDAISM

Henry Siegman
Executive Director
American Jewish Congress

Since our interfaith session is taking place on a Sunday morning, I should perhaps alert you at the outset that I do not intend this as an exercise in Sunday morning interfaith sentimentality, a widespread phenomenon in this country in the '40's and '50's. Known as the Brotherhood Movement, it was characterized primarily by its theological shallowness and lack of ecumenical seriousness. My remarks are not intended to be provocative, but neither are they falsely irenic.

There are troubling questions that need to be raised if our quest for peace and justice is to be taken seriously. Raising these questions will perhaps put me at odds with respected colleagues. I console myself with the Talmudic assurance that *kinat sofrim tarbeh chocmah* (the conflict of scholars increases knowledge).

Before I touch on the questions that I find so deeply troubling, I will make a few brief theoretical observations regarding the relationship of Judaism to our subject — transnationalism.

Like Christianity and Islām, Judaism is inherently "transnational", in the narrow but nevertheless fundamental sense that it demands a commitment to a set of beliefs and values that transcend the authority of the State and its political boundaries. It is generally assumed that Judaism is less transnational — if one can put it that way — than Christianity and Islām because of its pronounced particularism, a particularism expressed not only in the concept of Jewish peoplehood — a concept which, after all, Vatican II reclaimed for the Church, and Islām always retained in the notion of the *ummah* — but by what is called in the Harvard Seminar Papers "the territorial principle" — that is to say, the connection of Judaism to a particular geography, the land of Israel. It is in contrast to this "territorialism" that Christianity and

63

Islām have traditionally affirmed their own universalism.

I suggest to you that in this notion of Judaism as a less-than-transnational brand of religion we have an interesting example of how history can play havoc with theory. For most of their history, both Christianity and Islām lived in states that were at least nominally, and quite often if fact, either Christian or Muslim. Jews, on the other hand, have lived for most of their history in states that were not Jewish. Indeed, for the most part, they lived in states whose hostility to Judaism was so intense as to jeopardize the very existence of the Jewish people and the Jewish faith. Even today, with the creation of the State of Israel, a majority of Jews live in countries that are at least nominally Christian. This is likely to remain the Jewish situation for the foreseeable future.

What I am suggesting, therefore, is that the historical experience of Judaism, despite its putative particularism, has inclined it towards transnationalism, while the historial experience of Christianity and Islām, despite their putative universalism, has been that of particularism.

The notion of religious faith demanding a loyalty transcending all other loyalties, including national loyalties, was not shaped solely by the exigencies of Jewish diaspora existence. It was a sensibility made explicit in and nourished by early bibilical writings and the exhortation of the prophets of Israel. Thus, the author of Deuteronomy (17: 18-20) outlines the duties of the king as follows:

And it shall be, when he sitteth upon the throne of his kingdom, that he shall write him a copy of the Torah in a scroll, out of that which is before the priests the Levites. And it shall be with him, and he shall read therein all the days of his life; that he may learn to fear the Lord his God, to keep all the words of this Law and these statutes, to do them; that his heart be not lifted up above his brethren, and that he turn not aside from the commandment, to the right hand, or to the left ...

The prophetic writings proclaiming loyalty to God and the commandments of His Torah, and the pursuit of justice and righteousness as taking precedence over loyalty to king and country are too familiar to require elaboration. Indeed, the prophets of Israel proclaimed that God rejects even the cultic practices of Jewish faith if there is no social justice. Thus, in Isaiah 57, the prophet declares:

Daily they seek me, desiring to know my ways,
Asking me about righteous ordinances ...
But your fasting is amidst contention and strife ...
Can such be my chosen fast, the day of man's self-denial? ...
Is that what you call fasting, a day acceptable to the Lord?
Behold, this is the fast I decree precious
Loosen the chains of wickedness, undo the bonds of oppression,

Let the crushed go free, break all yokes of tyranny.
Share your food with the hungry, take the poor to your house
Clothe the naked, never turn from your fellow man.

Furthermore, Israel's territorial principle — its link to the land — was defined in an extraordinary way. Rather than demanding an absolute loyalty to that land, along the lines of modern nationalism, or of such atavistic notions as "blood and soil", the prophets of Israel developed the peculiar notion that the land itself was imbued with a transcendent intolerance of injustice and, therefore, would "vomit" — to use the biblical term — its own people and send them into exile if they violated the Torah's commandments. Thus, Israel's territorial principle paradoxically made for a supreme form of transnationalism, rather than the reverse.

Let me now go from these brief theoretical considerations — much of it, I grant you, in the tradition of religious apologetics — to some of the more practical problems of history. What history suggests is that if faith communities possess resources that are uniquely conducive to world community, these resources are, in fact, latent, suppressed and neutralized in our respective traditions. It will not do to insist that religions are, by definition, a power for peace in the world, and that divisive conflicts engendered by religious passions are to be blamed on the inability of the believers to live up to the high ideals of their respective faiths. As Wilfred Cantwell Smith said in a paper delivered at the Bellagio Conference,

We are haunted by an awareness of the devastation that we human beings have wrought in the name of God ... at least we *should* be haunted; the awareness *should* be stark, although self-righteousness has also been a besetting sin of the religious person or group, and each of us has often written and read a history that justifies our own community and is blind to the treatment of others.

Smith goes on to say that the problem is not an aberration from religious ideals. "It is inherent in them, a function of them, central to them. Divisiveness is not a failure of the religious (as we have inherited our traditions), but an ingredient of its success ... for a virtue of our religious faith is that it binds persons together into partial wholes."

It would, therefore, be hypocritical for religions to offer their unscrutinized resources as the great hope in the quest for transnationalism. There is much soul searching and much repentance that must take place before we offer ourselves as models to the world.

Let me begin by pointing to troubling evidence to support such skepticism from developments in my own religous community. It is a sad but inescapable fact that traditional religious influence has been most pronounced not in those forces in the State of Israel seeking

65

accommodation and compromise, but in the strident nationalism of Gush Emunim — which literally means "the block of the faithful." Their religous zealotry wishes to invest political institutions and geographical boundaries with an absolute religious sanctity that is impervious to the normal give-and-take of the political process in secular history.

It is true, of course, that the unity of faith, land and people is fundamental to Jewish identity and existence. But, as I have argued elsewhere (*Moment Magazine*, January 1976), there is a critical distinction to be made between the religious meaning to be appropriated from history, from temporal events, and imbuing these events with an absolute sacredness that removes them from the realm of history. The latter is Jewishly uncharacteristic, and leads to a chauvinism that is oblivious to the rights and the humanity of other people. In Jewish theological terms, it becomes *avodah zarah* — idolatry. I, therefore, consider the views of Gush Emunim a perversion of normative Judaism. However, the impact of religion on the affairs of men must finally be measured not by the apologetics of theologians, but by how the faithful act in history.

If I am distressed by the excesses of some of my co-religionists in Israel, I am appalled by recent expressions of Islāmic renaissance — in Libya, Pakistan and Iran. I do not wish to join the debate of whether or not the deposed Shah is to be compared to Hitler. Clearly, he is responsible for much evil and much suffering, even if the comparison to Hitler is entirely inappropriate. But, surely, he is not more evil than Idi Amin of Uganda, who was offered asylum by Kaddafi of the Islāmic Republic of Libya. I am not aware that Ayatollah Khomeini and the militants who are holding the hostages in the American embassy in Tehran were outraged by Kaddafi's action. Indeed, to this day, they seem entirely untroubled that Islāmic hospitality has prevented justice from reaching the butcher of Uganda.

At the risk of seeming to make self-serving distinctions, I must say that as aggrieved as I am by the intolerance of Gush Imunim, its extremism is redeemed by the criticism levelled against them from within the Jewish community itself, including the religious community. In a communication to the Prime Minister, Uri Simon, head of a religious peace movement in Israel (Oz Veshalom), wrote as follows:

> We as Jews committed to the Torah and to the observance of its precepts, feel ourselves duty bound to join with those who have called upon you at this critical hour to continue the full momentum of the efforts toward peace, and to prevent any irresponsible actions from undermining this pursuit.

> We are commanded by the Torah "to seek peace and to pursue it", and we are convinced that commitment to the holiness of the land does not conflict with our aspirations for peace with the Arabs, on

the basis of a reasonable compromise. Neither those extremist voices raised amongst us, nor those with little faith in the prospects for peace, represent the views of many who are faithful to the Torah of Israel.

Yehoshafat Harkabi, a former chief of military intelligence in Israel and more recently an advisor to the Prime Minister, warns in the *Jerusalem Post* (November 15) that attempts to annex the West Bank will lead to a "profound moral and spiritual crisis."

In 1970, 350 reserve officers and combat soldiers wrote to Prime Minister Begin the following letter:

We write to you out of the deepest concern. A government that will prefer the existence of Israel in borders of the greater Israel to its existence in peace in the context of good neighborly relations will arouse in us grave misgivings. A government that will prefer the establishment of settlements across the "green line" to the ending of the historic conflict and to the establishment of a system of moral relations will raise questions about the justice of our course. A government policy that will lead to the continued rule over one million Arabs is liable to damage the Jewish democratic character of the state, and would make it difficult for us to identify with the basic direction of the State of Israel.

We are fully aware of the security requirements of the State of Israel and the difficulties that lie on the path to peace. Nonetheless, we know that true security will be achieved only with the advent of peace. The strength of the Israel Defence Forces lies in the identification of its soldiers with the course of the State of Israel.

Out of this letter grew Israel's Peace Now movement, a powerful moral and religious force in Israel for compromise and conciliation.

If there are similar correctives to Islāmic extremism within the Islāmic religious community, I am unaware of them. I am also unaware, for that matter, of any criticism of Saudi policies which, in the name of Islām, deny Jews and Christians the right to worship publicly in that country, and whose religious leaders disseminate such classic anti-Semitic tracts as the "Protocols of the Elders of Zion."

In the paper prepared for the Harvard Seminar by Professor Ismā'īl al Fārūqī, one reads that "The Ummah is a world order whose essence is peace and the renunciation of war and conflict. Its cardinal principles are the free movement of humans (no passports and no visas), and the free movement of ideas (no curtains — may the best argument win), and the free movement of labor." Even the strictest observance of ecumenical etiquette cannot suppress the question, where in the Islāmic world do these sublime conditions obtain: in Libya? In Iran? In Saudi Arabia?

What characterizes the Islāmic world order is the precise reverse of the conditions described by al Fārūqī: relentless war and conflict; rejoicing by the Ayatollah over the sacking of the U.S. Embassy in Pakistan and its attendant loss of life; repression of unorthodox ideas; restrictions on the movement of peoples (e.g. Jews in Syria), etc. Surely, there comes a point when the gap between apologetics and reality is so horrendous as to end meaningful communication.

The Harvard Seminar addressed the question of the "legitimacy role" of religion. In his summary of the discussion, Msgr. Joseph Gremillion notes correctly that no serious effort was made to define the meaning of that term. As one reads the summary of the proceedings, one gets the uncomfortable feeling that this "legitimacy role" is determined by a faith community's association with and support of certain social, economic and political objectives, which happen to coincide, more or less, with the Third World's agenda. That, it seems to me, is a highly problematic proposition. Can the legitimacy of religious faith be determined by criteria external to that faith? The most serious criticism of religion in modern times is its propensity to ideology — a propensity that compromises its integrity and credibility. Uncritical acceptance of the Third World's presumption to a superior morality, far from attesting to the "legitimacy role of relgion", is an abandonment of that role.

I readily admit that it is a seemingly narrow Jewish concern that prompts this observation. On September 7, 1979 the heads of state of 89 non-aligned countries, at their meeting in Havana, issued a 130-page statement which declares Zionism a crime against humanity. Forty years after Aushwitz the non-aligned countries of the world have stopped just short — but by very much — of declaring it a crime against humanity to be a Jew. If our religious transnational actors for peace and justice found this declaration obscene, or even discomforting, they have shown remarkable restraint.

Actually, the issue is not all "narrow" or particularistic. For one thing, a universalism that has no tolerance for discreet particularisms can easily be transformed into a demonic force, a lesson we have learned only too well. Furthermore, the declaration is reprehensible not only for what it has to say about Zionism, but because of its pro-totalitarian and anti-democratic character. Indeed, it is an unrelenting and malevolent attack on democratic nations and democratic values. Surely, transnational actors for peace and justice must have something to say about the injustice of totalitarian systems.

Such subservience to ideology — even Third World ideology — undermines the credibility of religious faith as a unifying force in world affairs. Of course, secular forms of community that are offered as substitutes for religious ones are even more deceptive. As Wilfred

Cantwell Smith observed, the only way to transcend the limited loyalties of our fragmented society is through a transcendence that is greater and more serious, not one that is less. There are those who maintain that only religious faith is capable of providing such transcendence, of engendering and sustaining that larger vision without which a new world community will never come into being. I no longer know whether they are right. Perhaps sufficient to our task is the conviction that religious faith can be *a* force, if not the *only one*, germane to this task. At the very least, those who speak in the name of religion must not make the task more difficult than it is.

CHAPTER 9
THE FAITH COMMUNITY AND WORLD ORDER: THE PERSPECTIVE OF CHRISTIANITY

James Finn
Vice-President
Council on Religion and International Affairs

To speak comprehensively of the Christian community as a transnational actor is to speak of a far-flung network of approximately 1,100 million people who give allegiance to one of four major groups: the Orthodox churches, the Roman Catholic Church, the Protestant churches of the Reformation, and the Evangelical "Free"churches. But it is difficult to speak both comprehensively and incisively in brief compass. Constraints of time and competence instruct me to limit the scope of this address. I am, therefore, going to concentrate my comments on the Roman Catholic Church as it has addressed specific issues of peace and justice within the last two decades.

In speaking of the Church as a transnational actor, I am going to follow a clear but not yet beaten path marked out by Ivan Vallier and J. Bryan Hehir. In 1971, Vallier analyzed the international activities of the Church as one would analyze those of any large organization. The method was original and his findings revealed and clarified much that traditional description had left in obscurity. The description was sufficiently flattering to the Church as a transnational actor that representatives of other transnational enterprises, i.e., multinational corporations, occasionally said they wished their own organizations were run as competently and efficiently — and sometimes they were serious.

In terms of international affairs, the most visible and important units on which the Church depends include the Holy See (the papacy), the body of bishops, the clergy, and the areas (dioceses) in which they operate; the various religious orders; the members of the Church, approximately 650 million in number. Elements of these units are joined in many complex and often overlapping ways to perform specialized tasks. Frequently too, they join with other groups outside the Catholic Church, some of which are religious, some of which are not. In terms of formal international relations, the Vatican diplomatic corps has a unique role. In virtue of its juridic personality, the Holy See maintains through its diplomatic corps relations with over 100 countries around the world. In addition, the Holy See is active diplomatically in most agencies of the United Nations, which it has strongly supported from its inception, in the European Economic Community, the European Conference on Security and Cooperation, and in forums on such different issues as the Middle East and nuclear proliferation.

Although Vallier brought an untraditional method of analysis to bear on these structures, he accepted the general and historical view that in international affairs the policies to be followed were generated and controlled almost exclusively by the central authority of the Church located in the Vatican.

Giving full credit to the originality and usefulness of Vallier's description of the Church as a transnational actor, J. Bryan Hehir found it deficient in two significant ways: "First, it failed to provide any sense of the 'ideological' (theological) foundation which sustains and legitimizes the action of the church in world affairs; second, the analysis of dynamics within the church concentrated too exclusively on the flow from the center (Rome) to the periphery (local or national churches)."[2]

Accepting Vallier's functional description of the Church with Hehir's significant modifications, one can describe the Church as a transnational actor in virtue of its internal organization, of its relations with other institutions, of its activities and with an overall purpose in which it perceives its own cause for being. That purpose, which it shares to a large extent with other Christian bodies, at the heart of which it perceives a mystery, has been and will continue to be variously described. In words particularly appropriate to our concerns, one of the major documents of Vatican Council II, the *Dogmatic Constitution on the Church*, said: "The conditions of this age lend special urgency to the Church's task of bringing all men to full union with Christ, since mankind today is joined together more closely than ever before by social, technical, and cultural bonds."[3]

Against this background, I am going to trace the ways in which, during recent decades and up to this very moment, the Church has coped with specific questions of war and peace and with specific questions of human rights.

I. War and Peace
    A. Conscientious Objection
    The Church has a long, highly developed tradition of teaching about

war, but in the last several decades major tenets have been severely tested by (1) questions concerning the conscience of the individual Christian who is faced with politically and morally complex decisions about modern war, (2) by the threat of massive destruction posed by nuclear weapons at one end of a scale of violence, and (3) by "revolutionary" acts of terrorism at the other end of the scale. There has always existed within the Church a tradition of pacifism that has nourished and been nourished by Catholic pacifists. But compared to the robust tradition of just war teaching it has seemed thin and insubstantial. It is not surprising, then, that with less than complete accuracy pacifism has been commonly associated with the "peace churches" and the just war tradition with Catholicism.

The difficulties encountered over the years by Catholics whose consciences led them to pacifism were considerable. For example, Pius XII was known as the Pope of Peace and his motto was *Opus Justitiae Pax* (Peace, the Work of Justice). But in his Christmas Message of 1956 he stated that when under prescribed conditions a government engages in war, "a Catholic citizen cannot invoke his own conscience in order to refuse to serve and fulfill those duties the law imposes."⁴ In this country, the highly respected theologian John Courtney Murray understood this to mean that "the Pope of Peace has disallowed the validity of conscientious objection."⁵ In other countries, authoritative spokesmen within the Church read the text in the same way. This dampened but it did not suppress the work of Catholic pacifists, and when John XXIII issued *Pacem in Terris* in 1963, they were quick to detect the new tone struck in that encyclical. That document, which aroused world-wide attention, did not specifically allow conscientious objection, but the way in which it criticized the arms race and directed attention to structural defects in international relations led many people to believe that it lent support to the pacifist position. Within the context of their gospel belief, Catholic pacifists in many countries were further encouraged to develop the theological and moral bases of their position.

Explicit recognition and a degree of support for conscientious objection was to come just a few years later in one of the major documents of Vatican II, *Gaudium et Spes* (1965), which stated:

"It seems right that laws make provisions for the case of those who for reasons of conscience refuse to bear arms, provided however, that they accept some other form of service to the human community."⁶

Since 1965 the implications of that sentence have been explored in a number of statements by Paul VI, by the various Commissions of Justice and Peace established after Vatican II in conformity with the expressed desire of the Council Fathers, by episcopal conferences in many countries, by theologians, by those concerned with public policies and, of course, by many Catholic pacifists. In the course of that exploration, support for conscientious objection strengthened. The Synod of Bishops meeting in 1971 said: "Let a strategy of non-violence be fostered also, and let conscientious objection be recognized and regulated by law in each nation." And a few years later Cardinal Maurice Roy reported in his reflections on *Pacem in Terris* that military conscientious objection is a new right which now has legal status in many countries. As a consequence of this history, the Church's teaching on matters of war is more explicitly pluralist, richer and more complex than it was when Pope John XXIII assumed the papacy in 1958.

In this process of extending its teaching on war, the Church acted as a transnational actor in several respects. It drew upon the wisdom of individuals and organizations of many countries and it formulated a statement applicable to individuals and policies of many countries. The process was also one that drew upon the reflections and judgment of people at different levels of authority within the Church, many of whom grounded their positions in the gospel message.

Conscientious objection to all wars is a natural corollary to pacifism and is so recognized in the policies of a number of countries. Selective conscientious objection might be regarded as the natural corollary of a tradition that distinguishes between wars that are justifiable and those that are not. It is historically true that it was not so regarded either in the teachings of the Church or the laws of this country. The ferment within the Church and the war in Vietnam combined to force a reexamination of just war principles as they applied to matters of the individual conscience and of public policy. These exigencies led the Catholic bishops of the United States to issue in 1968 a pastoral letter on "Human Life in Our Day" in which they reflected on the threat that present military arsenals level at the family of nations. In the course of their reflections, they said:

"If war is ever to be outlawed, and replaced by more humane and enlightened institutions to regulate conflicts among nations, institutions rooted in the notion of universal common good, it will be because the citizens of this and other nations have rejected the tenets of exaggerated nationalism and insisted on principles of non-violent political and civic action in both the domestic and international spheres."[7]

Proceeding to specifics, the bishops then praised those who for reasons of conscience followed the path of non-violence and expressed support for laws that provide for those who totally reject the use of military force. The bishops then went further; they recommended legal provisions "making it possible, though not easy, for so-called selective conscientious objectors to refuse — without fear of imprisonment or loss of citizenship — to serve in wars which they consider unjust or in branches of service (e.g., the strategic nuclear forces) which would subject them to the performance of actions contrary to deeply held moral convictions about indiscriminate killing."* The bishops thus brought to bear on the existing public policies of this country — and by extension on other countries — the weight of principles elaborated over many centuries. In terms of conscientious objection to war, the principles of both pacifism and the just war tradition were made applicable to national policies.

B. Nuclear Weapons Systems

There can be no doubt that the urgency and even passion that invests papal, conciliar and other ecclesiastical statements on modern war stem from the realization of the enormous threat nuclear weapons pose to everyone on earth. In their eventual disposition, we are all involved. It is also true that these weapons pose moral and political problems that have so far seemed intractable.

Pius XII, who gave sustained attention to modern warfare, limited the legitimate causes of war to the single one of defending one's own nation or that of others unjustly attacked. But even he did not place an absolute proscription on the use of nuclear weapons. And in 1959, John Courtney Murray stated as a moral imperative that "since nuclear war may be a necessity, it must be made a possibility." Vatican II substantially modified the terms of the discussion. In the only condemnation it issued, the Council asserted:

"Any act of war aimed indiscriminately at the destruction of entire cities or of extensive areas along with their population is a crime against God and man himself. It merits unequivocal and unhesitating condemnation.

"The unique hazard of modern warfare consists in this: it provides those who possess modern scientific weapons with a kind of occasion for perpetuating just abominations."⁹

The condemnation directed at the *use* of nuclear weapons was not extended to their *possession*. The Council explicitly recognized that many people regard nuclear deterrence "as the most effective way by which peace of a sort can be maintained between nations at the present time." Refraining from judgment on this issue, the Council continued: "Whatever be the case with this method of deterrence, men should be convinced that the arms race in which so many countries are engaged is not a safe way to preserve a steady peace."¹⁰ And again: "The arms race is an utterly treacherous trap for humanity, and one which injures the poor to an intolerable degree."

The policy of deterrence presents a limiting case to the traditional teaching of the Church and to all who would attempt to resolve it in coherent moral terms. Those who would do so must respond to the crucial question of whether it is morally acceptable to *threaten* an evil that it would be immoral to *accomplish*. And they must consider that question within a situation in which the removal of the threat could itself lead to a great evil. These are questions to be answered not only in abstract moral terms but in terms of public policy and practical decision.

The principal papal and episcopal comments on this question, while strongly critical of deterrence, have been properly cautious and tentative in suggesting alternatives. As late as May 1978, Pope Paul VI in his message to the U.N. special session on disarmament stated that the present balance of terror must be replaced by a balance of trust. But he added that solid international trust "presupposes structures that are objectively suitable for guaranteeing, by peaceful means, security and respect for or recognition of everyone's right against always possible bad will."

There is one major exception to, one notable departure from, the mainstream of such authoritative reflections. In 1976, the Catholic bishops of the United States warned that "With respect to nuclear weapons, at least those with massive, destructive capability, the first imperative is to prevent their use." They then proceeded to make an extraordinary judgment: "As possessors of a vast nuclear arsenal, we must also be aware that not only is it wrong to attack civilian populations, but it is also wrong to threaten to attack them as part of a strategy of deterrence."[11] The deep explication this statement demands for it to be fully intelligible is yet to be made. In the meantime, the superpowers depend upon mutual deterrence systems to sustain the present equilibrium.

C. Revolution and Terrorism

If nuclear weapons pose seemingly intractable moral problems at one end of the scale, acts of terrorism do so at the other. The world has grown familiar in recent decades and recent years with revolutionaries, guerrillas, terrorists who have killed and injured innocent people, noncombatants in the traditional sense of that term. Each of these acts and each set of circumstances surrounding them must be examined before any moral judgment is possible. That we will be called upon to make such judgments frequently in coming years is almost inevitable. The Middle East, Africa, Asia and Latin America all have active liberation movements whose aims are presently unfulfilled. Pope Paul VI provided justification for some revolutionary acts when, in 1967, he spoke of the need for development in poor countries and warned of the terrible alternatives if it did not take place. In *Populorum Progressio*, he stated:

"There are certainly situations whose injustice cries to heaven. When whole populations destitute of necessities live in a state of dependence barring them from all initiative and responsibility, and all opportunity

76

to advance culturally and share in social and political life, recourse to violence as a means to right those wrongs to human dignity, is a grave temptation.

"We know, however, that a revolutionary uprising — save where there is manifest long-standing tyranny which would do great damage to the common good of the country — produces new injustices, throws more elements out of balance and brings on new disasters. A real evil should not be fought against at the cost of greater misery."[12]

This is clearly a caution against rash acts of violence conceived of as revolutionary. However, the interpolated clause concerning "long-standing tyranny" states the conditions under which revolutionary uprisings can justifiably occur. Whether those conditions exist must be determined on empirical grounds, and that determination can probably best be made by the people who are caught up in, who are suffering under, those conditions.

While the statement of Paul VI is general and universalizable, it probably received its warmest reception, at least initially, in Latin America. In the following year, the Second General Conference of Latin American Bishops held in Medellin, Colombia, made repeated references to *Populorum Progressio* and elaborated many of its themes. The Medellin documents, as the papers of that conference came to be known, provided both base and sustenance to a "theology of liberation." In the decade since Medellin, that theology has attracted the energies and substantial talents of many people and has burst out of the Latin American continent. In some of its manifestations, it justifies guerrilla warfare in terms that strain if they do not actually discard traditional teaching of what is justifiable in war. One Brazilian priest noted the "hunger, misery, unemployment, unjust wages, and lack of respect for human life" that were the daily burden of his people. Then, referring both to *Populorum Progressio* and the Medellin documents, he asserted: "Against this *state* of violence *acts* of violence are necessary to save humanity from slavery."

Attitudes such as these inspire liberation movements, guerrilla warfare and, at an extreme, acts of terrorism in countries around the globe. These manifestations of violence challenge the Christian community to appreciate the depth and intensity of concern that prompts these acts even as the community itself criticizes and opposes acts which escape the limits of justifiable war.

II. Human Rights

To turn from questions of war and peace to questions of human rights is not to make a leap as great as it might seem, for the two large issues of peace and human rights are inextricably intertwined. The document that made this indisputably clear in our time is, again, John XXIII's

Pacem in Terris. Several decades ago the term "human rights" did not have the currency it now has. It was certainly not a lively part of the Christian vocabulary, the concepts to which it refers being subsumed in Roman Catholic parlance under the general rubric of "natural rights of men and women." John XXIII made the breakthrough when in his encyclical he brought the modern development of human rights into conjunction with traditional Catholic thought. Calling the Universal Declaration of Human Rights that was proclaimed by the U.N. General Assembly in 1948 an act of the greatest importance, he numbered it among "the signs of the times" that we must discern in our efforts to achieve greater justice. For those reasons, *Pacem in Terris* has been called the first declaration on human rights made by papal authority. Whatever the merit of that description, the term human rights is now a significant part of the Catholic, the Christian vocabulary. It occurs in the documents of Vatican II, in messages of Paul VI, as we have recently observed, in major addresses of John Paul II. And it is closely tied to the demands of justice.

The relation between peace and justice is stated in general terms in *Gaudium et Spes:*

"Peace is not merely the absence of war. Nor can it be reduced solely to the maintenance of a balance of power between enemies. Nor is it brought about by dictatorship. Instead it is rightly and appropriately called 'an enterprise of justice' (Is. 32:7)."[13]

Fully aware, however, of the criticisms launched against the Church by those who accuse it of fostering injustice by counseling patience to the wretched and the deprived, the Council Fathers urged action in this world. They referred to "the birth of a new humanism, one in which man is defined primarily in terms of his responsibility for his brothers and for history." They called upon Christians to give witness to a faith that proves itself "by activating him toward justice and love, especially regarding the needy." "Faith must not weaken but rather stimulate our concern for cultivating this world."

Many of the major post-conciliar documents echoed and strengthened these sentiments with increasing specificity. Pope Paul VI noted that "today the principal fact that we must all recognize is that the social question has become world-wide." And in 1971, the College of Bishops meeting in Rome declared:

"Action on behalf of justice and participation in the transformation of the world fully appear to us as a constitutional dimension of the preaching of the Gospel, or, in other words, of the Church's mission for the redemption of the human race and its liberation from every oppressive situation."[14]

For the Catholic Church, it is apparent, the issue of human rights has opened out to the world scene in which it is a transnational actor — but only *an* actor. From Pope John XXIII to John Paul II, the Church has increasingly acknowledged its limitations as well as its responsibilities as it operates in the social order. On the international scene, the economic and political problems seem almost as intractable as those posed by the weapons of modern warfare. It is clear that many transnational actors must work together to deal with these problems and the possibility that the Catholic community can work ever more closely with other Christian communities, and Christian communities with other faith communities of the Book is encouraging. But I do not wish to end on that optimistic note, tentative as it is. I would rather call attention to the way that John Paul II drew together issues of peace and human rights when he spoke at the United Nations on October 2, 1979, and to the way in which his approach to human rights transcended an approach that pits political and civil rights against economic and social rights.

Referring to the Universal Declaration of Human Rights, the Pope asserted that it "has struck a real blow against the many roots of war, since the spirit of war, in its basic primordial meaning, springs up and grows to maturity where the inalienable rights of man are violated."

These rights exist in both the material and spiritual order, and "any threat to human rights, whether in the field of material realities or in that of spiritual realities, is equally dangerous for peace, since in every instance it concerns man in his entirety." This does not deny, however, the preeminence of spiritual values, since they define the proper "sense of earth material goods and the way to use them."

There exist is the modern world two main threats, John Paul said. The first is linked to the uneven distribution of goods within and between countries, to the disparity between the very rich and the very poor, to the deprivation of those material goods without which it is impossible to develop as full human persons. The second threat is directed at the field of the spirit, for "man can indeed be wounded in his inner relationship with truth, in his conscience, in his most personal belief, in his view of the world, in his religious faith, and in the sphere of what are known as civil liberties." Everyone, in every nation, under any political system should be free to enjoy these rights.

John Paul II spoke as the head of the Catholic Church to the assembly of the world's nations. He was the personification of the Church as a transnational actor. But his statements, like all that are necessarily elevated to a high level of generality, must be applied to a variety of differing local, national and regional situations. They must be interpreted and implemented by people with different degrees of authority, different disciplines, different cultures, different talents and, it must be acknowledged, with different degrees of agreement with his presentation. Within the Church, this will mean a flow of intentional activity, not only from the top down or the center out, but between the many actors and agencies within the Church. It will also increasingly mean cooperative efforts between the Church and other faith communities. For an overview of the Church during the last two decades shows that it has moved into the economic and political realities of our time with increasing humility and determination.

NOTES

1. Ivan Vallier. "The Roman Catholic Church: A Transnational Actor." *Transnational Relations in World Politics*, R.O. Keoham and J.S. Nye, eds. (Cambridge, 1972).
2. J. Bryan Hehir, "The Roman Catholic Church as Transnational Actor: Amending Vallier," paper presented at the 19th Annual Convention of the International Studies Association, February, 1978.
3. "Dogmatic Constitution on the Church" in *The Documents of Vatican II*, Walter Abbott, S.J., ed. (New York, 1966), paragraph 1, p. 15.
4. Cited in *Morality and Modern War*, John Courtney Murray, S.J. (New York, 1959), pp. 14-15.
5. *Ibid.* p. 14.
6. *Documents of Vatican II*, op. cit., 79, p. 292.
7. *Human Life in Our Day*, issued November 15, 1968, by United States Catholic Conference (Washington, D.C., 1968), p. 43.
8. *Gaudiam et Spes*, in *Documents of Vatican II*, 80, p. 294.
9. *Ibid.*
10. *Ibid.*, 81, pp. 294-95.
11. *To Live in Christ Jesus*, United States Catholic Conference (Washington, D.C., 1976), p. 14.
12. *Populorum Progressio* in *The Gospel of Peace and Justice*, Joseph Gremillion, ed. (New York, 1976), 31, p. 396.
13. *Ibid.* 78, p. 290.
14. "Justice in the World," in Gremillion, op. cit., 6, p. 514.

CHAPTER 10
THE FAITH COMMUNITY AND WORLD ORDER
IN THE PERSPECTIVE OF ISLĀM

Maḥmūd 'Awān
Professor of Management
Nichols College

I. The Human Need for World Order

During a ceremony at the Swedish International Peace Research Institute on May 11, 1979, the late Earl Mountbatten of Burma said:

There have been numerous international conferences and negotiations on the subject and we have all nursed dreams of the world at peace but to no avail. Since the end of the Second World War, 34 years ago, we have had war after war... There are powerful voices around the world who still give credence to the old Roman precept — if you desire peace, prepare for war. This is absolute nuclear nonsense. I repeat, it is a disastrous misconception to believe that by increasing the total uncertainty one increases one's own certainty. It is true after all that science offers us almost unlimited opportunities but it is up to us, the people, to make the moral and philosophical choices and since the threat to humanity is the work of human beings, it is up to man to save himself from himself. [1]

In an era of unprecedented nuclear terror and blackmail, perils of war need no undue emphasis. We are all witnesses to this climate of mounting uncertainty where every day brings in new anxieties and fears that inexorably turn into harsh reality of total human insecurity. The world has long adjusted to the possibilities of some form of conflict or tension in random spots. But is it now getting ready to adjust itself to nuclear arsenals proliferation and the development of laser and particle beam weapons that will make even ICB missiles rather obsolete? Has the world accepted as its fate the inevitability of nuclear warfare which will leave no spot on this planet unscathed? Are the nation-states of this world resigned to the eventuality of mutual destruction? Or, are they willing to search for alternatives to this grim yet avoidable scenario of total annihilation? There are no unequivocal or definite answers to these questions. Peace, though theoretically attainable, does not lend itself well to simple conceptualizations. Its link with problems of international justice, fair play, rule of law, and protection of human rights nevertheless is quite obvious. Together, they make the search for peace so rewarding and meaningful. It is not a search in vain.

Control of the world's limited economic and natural resources has long been a favorite preoccupation of nation-states. The desire to accumulate and exploit these resources to the exclusion of other nation-states has historically been a major source of international conflict; propensity to control productive resources has often led to the exercise of military and political power even in our own times. Military expansionism and colonization motivated by the desire to monopolize resources has understandably caused widespread injustice and discontent. To the extent that nation-states seek and get legitimacy from religion to carry out such operations, problems of injustice become even more complex and probably longer lasting.

The formerly colonized nations of the world have only recently begun to understand the extent of hardship and injustice caused to them by their colonizers. this recognition has taken many forms. It has been expressed in the world forums in very civilized patterns, but it has gone unnoticed. This deliberate neglect on the part of neo-colonizers has been pushing the oppressed peoples of the third world to radicalism and violent action. Simultaneously, in spite of their mighty military postures, the technologically advanced nations of the world are beginning to realize that their eco-military systems are very vulnerable. So are their moral and political positions.

II. Religion as Contender for World Order

Mutual dependence for economic and political survival has led to a renewed search for commonalities among nations. The Trialogue of the Abrahamic Faiths is an auspicious beginning which must be extended so as to include the faith-communities of the whole world. Over fifty percent of our planet's people do not believe in Abrahamic Faiths yet their destinies are intertwined with those of the believers. They too are becoming cognizant of the fact that the future wars will utilize arsenals that will hardly distinguish the fate of believers from non-believers. Nuclear technology and war planning executed in outer space cannot possibly guarantee one group's survival to the exclusion or at the expense of the other.

Thus the motivation for peace and justice in the modern world has to be on truly global scale. There is no place here for any particularism; and any ethnocentric claim must be ruled out *ex hypothesi*. The

82

criterion to judge the effectiveness and legitimacy of all claims is the universal benefit any claim promises to all the peoples. Such a criterion may seem commonplace, but history is replete with examples in which religion had a negative impact on peace and justice, created political and military conflicts, and/or blessed economic exploitation, political oppression, and persecution of the masses of adherents of another religion. Langdon Gilkey covers this dimension in the context of the political dimensions of Christian theology:

> "No King but was in the end divinely established; no ruler but sought and received the blessing of communal religion. The eighteenth century saw clearly this essential relation of religion, privilege and monarchy and the nineteenth the relation of religion and society's oppressive superstructure. But both thought that it had been a conspiracy of organized religion, especially of Christianity, that had imported this religious dimension into a potentially secular and so innocent politics. The twentieth century has shown on the contrary that ideology, a religious interpretation of and allegiance to a community's social mythos, springs up inexorably in all politics; that the divine legitimation of rule and the sacral character of a way of life — whether it be a Marxist or a liberal, capitalist ideology — is as much a character of advanced contemporary societies as was the union of religion, myth and kingship in a traditional society... The social myths of ethos that make our common life possible have a religious dimension. This is the source of the community's creativity, courage and confidence; it is also the ground of the demonic in historical life — of blind fanaticism, of infinite arrogance, of imperial ambition, of unlimited cruelty and of ultimate violence."[2]

The history of Islām presents us with no such phenomena as those of Judaism and Christianity. There is nothing comparable to the history of Judaism, where a diametrical reversal has taken place: namely, from being the most persecuted and tyrannized-over minority in Europe, to becoming the perpetrators of genocide against the Palestinians. To this, history adds the irony that Jewish fury and resentment are directed not against their former persecutors — the Nazis, Fascists and communists of Europe — but against the innocent Palestinians whose crime in Jewish eyes is that of having lived in Palestine for millennia before and after the Hebrews had established themselves in the territory for a comparatively brief period of its long history. The irony is double when we consider that religiously and culturally, the Palestinians are an integral part of the *ummah* which alone in the whole of human history, acknowledged Judaism as divine religion, its Torah as the Law of

God, and welcomed and protected the Jews wherever Islām was dominant. The cries of Palestinian victims massacred in cold blood by Jewish hands claiming to actualize the promise of the ethnocentric god, must have caused the Prophets of *ethical* monotheism to turn in their graves, as well as the geniuses of Islāmic-Jewish cooperation across the last fourteen centuries (Samuel ibn Nagdala and Ḥasdai ibn Shaprut, Moses Maimonides and Solomon ben Gabirol, Saadia Gaon Fayyūmī and Ḥayyūy ibn Zakarīyā, etc. etc.).

III. The Islamic Perspective

The perspective of Islām as regard the faith community and world order is not merely a matter of theology. It is not a deduction from the nature of God or that of the faith. Nor is it an eschatological hope entertained by the faithful, as an imaginary projection born out of frustration in space-time. It is not the "kingdom of God" conceived as an alternative to this-world which the religion declares to be fallen and hopeless. Nor is it a messianic idea animating history while remaining outside of it. Finally, a world order based on peace and justice is not an ideal to be brought about by God's initiative and work, with man passively acquiescing and singing Hallelujah! Islām regards the bringing about of a world order based on peace and justice as man's supreme religious duty, to be effected in this world, this space and time, and as soon as possible. Moreover, the world order Islām envisages and actively seeks is to be brought about by humans through ethical as well as efficacious action here and now. It is not to depend upon the good will of humans but must be maintained by constant vigil and action. This realization of the absolute in history is girded and protected by the *sharī'ah*, or Islāmic law. Consequently, it does not depend upon the good will or diplomacy of any ruler, of any bill of legislation the ruler or the ruled may promulgate. The law is God-ordained. It has its own methodology of interpretation, its own mechanism for self-renewal. And it is valid for all space, for all time.

A. The Unity of Humanity

Humanity, in the view of Islām, is one. God created all humans of a single pair — Adam and Eve. He created them all equal in their creatureliness; i.e., they are all His servants, charged with actualizing all His will which He has revealed, and they are all capable and responsible. Nobody is excepted; nobody is absolved; nobody is privileged or chosen; nobody carries more or less of the burden than any other, or is responsible for the performance of another. Responsibility on the Day of Judgment is absolutely personal. This absolute egalitariansim and universalism Islām understands as the direct implication of *tawḥīd*

84

(divine unity, ultimacy and transcendence). To claim the contrary, as ethnocentrism does, is to threaten the divine unity. If humans were ontologically disparate, then God too, their Creator, must be more than one. It is inconceivable that God be absolutely one, when His human creatures do not all stand to Him in exactly the same relation. For God to have favorites is for Him to be unjust and discriminating. but God is indeed God; hence, all humans are one and equal.

God does choose the time and place to send His messages to humankind. Those who receive the message are obliged to actualize it in themselves and proclaim it to the others. If they do, they deserve merit in God's eye. If they don't, God will not be frustrated. He will exchange them for another, different people who will fulfill the message in their lives and those of others (Qur'ān 2:143, 213; 40:9; 47:38).

If, despite all this, God constituted humans into tribes and nations, He did so to help them identify one another. The circumstances of our physical features, our languages and customs, our cultures and mores, as well as our geographical distribution on earth (including our distribution in houses, streets, villages, cities and provinces) — all these are aids for mutual self-identification. "O Humans, We have created you of a single pair and constituted you into tribes and nations that you may identify one another Nobler in the eye of God is the more righteous" (Qur'ān 49:13). Or, it is possible to understand this verse as meaning to say that the purpose of ethnic differentiation is mutual help and cooperation, an instance of the opposite working for its opposite. Thus, Islām is at once free of the limitations the doctrine of "Chosen People" imposes upon the Jews, or the doctrine of *Imago Dei* imposes upon Christians. Islāmic history knows of one attempt by Jahm ibn Ṣafwān (of Tirmidh) to introduce the idea of predeterminism, in the second/eighth century. But he lost his case and his movement collapsed. Naturally, Islāmic egalitarianism and universalism do not preclude differentiation between humans on the basis of knowledge and wisdom, of capacity and patience, of piety and righteousness. But these are all acquired and acquirable. No one may be ruled out. Competition in God's vicegerency is free and open to all humans. And no man's knowledge or righteousness may be judged apriorily.

For its universalism, Islām provides a base in its theory of man. All humans, it holds, are born endowed with the sense for the sacred and for the moral. All are innately equipped with the capacity to discern and recognize God as One and Creator, as well as His will as the moral imperative. Islām thus presupposes a *religio naturalis* with which all humans are equally endowed. It relegates to history and nature all that separates man from man; and it exhorts all humans to return to this primordial source of knowledge and wisdom in which they all share. "Turn your face to the primordial religion [*religio naturalis*] as a *ḥanīf* [the pre-Islāmic righteous person]. That is the natural endowment of God bestowed upon all humans by virtue of birth; equally shared by all humans without discrimnation. That is the true and valuable religion" (Qur'ān 30:30).

In order to maintain the free highway to God open to all humans, Islām abolished sacraments as well as all other priestly functions. To reach God, humans need no medium. To receive His grace and forgiveness, they need no sacrament. He is near, all too near, ever-ready to receive anyone who comes to Him with a candid heart. So, no church and no priest can ever monopolize the access to God, can rule out or condition anyone's approach to Him (Qur'ān 2:186; 11:61; 26:89; 37:84). Likewise, it is every Muslim's duty to call all humans to Islām, to invite and warn all humans equally to enter into the community of faith. Islām cannot countenance the tacit ethnocentrism of those who claim to carry more of God's burden than others, restricting application of their law or rituals to themselves and absolving other from same. Nor does Islām tolerate the division of humans into castes, and declaring one caste expected to be monotheist, the other polytheist or idolatrous. Contrary to both varieties of particularism, Islām is a missionary religion requiring its adherents to offer and teach the divine message to all humans and to invite them all to join the faith. according to the Old Testament, the children of Jacob slew the Shechemites and robbed them of their goods because the latter offered to convert to the religion of Jacob (Genesis 34); and German racists would go to war if half a billion blacks or a billion Chinese were to declare themselves German. To the Muslim, the entrance of anyone or any group into Islām elicits one exclamation: *Allahu Akbar wa lillahi al ḥamd* (God is Greatest! To Him be the Praise!).

Islām therefore condemns nationalism and particularism as an evil aberration, unworthy of the wise and righteous. It seeks the universal community. Though it may start anywhere, the community and state of Islām are to expand so as to cover humanity and the whole of creation. This expansion, however, may not be achieved by force or violence. "No coercion in religion," God affirms in the Qur'ān; "the truth is manifestly other than error... Whoever wishes to believe let him do so; and whoever wishes to disbelieve let him do so" (Qur'ān 2:256; 18:29). It must be achieved, if at all, by sound reasoning and dialogue, by goodly exhortation (Qur'ān 16:125). Jews and Christians are to be invited by Muslims to rally with the Muslims around a fair principle, namely, not worship but God, not to associate aught with Him, and not to lord it over one another (Qur'ān 3:64). For what is sought is the moral — hence free — acquiescence to God, and His will and Messenger. A forced acquiescence is devoid of ethical value and merits for the enforcer the punishment of Hell. No Muslim may ask for any more than the freedom to call, to present the case of Islām for the understanding. The freedom to convince others of the truth, and the freedom to be convinced of the truth belongs essentially to humanity. Nobody may be deprived of this most basic human right. In the past, Muslims have gone to war — and rightly so — when their emissaries carrying nothing but the message of Islām were attacked or killed. Should the Jews and/ or Christians reject the message of Islām, no Muslim has the right to molest them in their practice of their religions. Equally, the call to God must be made for His own sake, in thorough candidness and honesty. The example of Christian missions colluding with colonialism, whether naively or deliberately, to exploit the sickness, poverty or weakness of Muslims must not only be stopped, but also never imitated.

The universal community is the noblest ideal humans have entertained for their association with one another. First, to be defined and identified in terms of that which one holds precious — indeed, of ultimate value — accords with human dignity and befits the cosmic role humans are to play in spacetime. To define oneself in terms of ethnic entity, of one's geography or other necessary accidents of birth, is too demeaning to humanity. Second, as adherents of their faiths, Jews, Christians and Muslims stand under one and the same God Whom they all acknowledge. This, after all, is the foundation of the Abrahamic faith to which they subscribe. Under that faith, God is the best Knower, the ultimate Judge. A fortiori, they ought to lay themselves eternally open to God's determination, acknowledge and tolerate one another in God's name. And yet, whereas Christianity regards Judaism as a mere preparation for itself and Islām as un-religion, Judaism regards both Christianity and Islām as heresies. Only Islām regards both Judaism and Christianity as itself, viz., as religions of God and their scriptures as divine revelation. Certainly Islām is critical of the two sister faiths, but no more than they have been of themselves. In their religious controversies with one another, Islām is willing to let the best and true argument win. Thirdly, if communication and spiritual intercourse between their adherents is desirable, then there should be no curtains and no censorship. To isolate a community from the truth under the pretext that humans are unable to make up their minds intelligently and responsibly is an insult to humanity at large. Equally, to subvert the free and responsible exchange of ideas with bribes, to exploit the sickness and weakness of humans in order to compel them to convert so as to receive the desired aid, is criminal. Fourthly, once it is recognized that human association is to be based on faith, and that the faiths of mankind are guaranteed by the constitution, there would be no justification for the fragmentation of the world in nation-states in competition with one another. Just as Caliph 'Umar ibn al Khaṭṭāb (RAA) ordered all customs and immigration barriers removed from within the Islāmic world-state, the globe too could well be a place in which humans may choose their residences in total freedom. Why may not the Jews reside in Palestine, the Japanese in Berlin, and the Chinese in Chicago if they wish to and seek to establish such residence without aggression or injustice? And why may they not import and export their wealth and other goods as they please, and without customs?

Certainly, the demography and economy of the various regions will change in consequence of such unification of the planet earth. Buy why should they not do so? Only ethnocentrism, the egotistic pursuit of a nation's welfare regardless of cost to humanity — indeed *pereat mundus* — answers that the national demography and economy should not change. But the universal community is a sublime value, a value associated with the will of the transcedent Creator, a value which ethnocentric particularism cannot even understand.

B. The World Order as Pax Islamica

Ethnocentrism and nationalism necessarily lead to war. In his address of yesterday [*supra*, Chap. 7], Professor al Fārūqī has made the distinction of ethnocentrism/nationalism from patriotism evidently clear. Ethnocentrism/nationalism would not only be harmless if all it meant was patriotism, but it would even be a virtue. In fact, ethnocentrism/nationalism presupposes as an absolute axiom that the good of the ethnic/national group has priority over the good of all others. This priority is the essential distinguishing characteristic. Without it, ethnocentrism/nationalism would not be itself. It would not close its doors in face of those who wish to join the ethnic group; nor would it define membership of the group in terms of birth and physical characteristics. Its law would be, at least as far as it is concerned, the law for all humans. It would be a free society open to whosoever wishes to subscribe to it. It would not differentiate between humans as to treatment and would treat the stranger who comes under its jurisdiction equally as the citizen/adherent. Discrimination between the members/adherents and others, preferential treatment by God, the state, or both of the "chosen," pursuit of the welfare of the members at the cost of others, are necessary practices of the nation-state. That is the meaning of "priority" axiomatically predicated of the members' welfare. "Priority" is a comparative concept and would be meaningless without an "other" to whom the member is preferred, against whom the member's welfare is sought. This is the core of all the nationalist and colonialist wars which characterized the nation-state from its origins to the present day. In a world populated exclusively by the members of one ethnic/national group, ethnocentrism/nationalism would be meaningless; and the nation-state would be indistinguishable from any other kind of state.

Islām identifies ethnocentrism/nationalism as the first and greatest source of social evil. It not only sets nation against nation; but within the same nation, it sets one class, one province, or one segment of the people against another. The conflicts it generates are infinite, as the occasions of life in which members of the ethnic/national group may be preferred to, or assigned priority over, the others are infinite. Whether in their pursuit of physical subsistence and economic well being, of cultural growth and development, of esthetic enjoyment or, finally, of religious adoration and service, ethnocentrism/nationalism is bound to aggress upon the rights of other humans, and incept hostilities. In so doing, it violates the dignity of humans as well as of God. Its eradication from the earth would stop the major source of war, and open the way for human unity.

The world order Islām envisages, therefore, is an order of peace where no ethnic group or nation would be in conflict with another. Humanity would continue to be arranged in continents, provinces and ethnic/national groups; but none would have the power to aggress upon another. Ethnicity/nationality would lose its importance because, in an Islāmic world order, it would play the insignificant role of identification. "Territory" or province, language group and community would in the Islāmic world order be merely a geographic, at best an administrative, category.

Under the *Pax Islamica*, humans would be categorized according to their religious adherence, i.e., according to what they regard as ultimate reality, ultimate meaning, ultimate function and place in space-time. Like the other religious groups including the Muslims, the Jews and Christians may order the lives of their members according to the dictates of their own tradition, as interpreted by their own institutions, and adjudicated by their own courts of law. Rebellion against Judaism and Christianity, against their laws and institutions, their legitimate representatives and functionaries, will not be tolerated. Islāmic law obliges the state to support the integrity of all the religions and their communities. Barring a few instances of mad rulers or governors, under whom Muslims suffered more than either Jews or Christians, Islāmic history knows of no case in which the integrity of Judaism or of Christiantiy was violated by the Islāmic state. Islāmic law regards such violation, or interference, as injustice and aggression. Any Islāmic court of law has jurisdiction to look into any case presented and deliver its verdict even if it indicts the Islāmic state itself.

The *Pax Islāmica* is indeed an order of peace. Armed conflict would be banned among its constituent religious communities, since their competition can go only in ideational matters. The best argument should and would win. Islām's world order is then a pluralistic order where pluralism is in the matter which really counts, namely, the laws by which human lives are ordered. There can be no more significant pluralism than in the laws. Unlike any other law, the *shari'ah* or law of Islam allows other legal systems to operate within its jurisdiction, without injury or prejudice to anyone, making the *Pax Islamica* a sort of legal federalism. While governing the lives of Muslims in all detail, the *shari'ah* orders the affairs of state in the *Pax Islamica*. Matters of public order within, of war and peace without, are governed exclusively by the *shari'ah*, thus maintaining the peace and integrity of the *Pax Islamica*.

Surely, humans may and will continue to sin, to plot and aggress upon one another. The world-state would interfere in order to put a stop to and undo the aggression. For this, a higher loyalty than to ethnic entity, person or interest group is necessary to animate, to inspire and drive the state. This cannot be other than faith in and loyalty to, God alone. Likewise, in arresting aggression and undoing injustice, the whole universal community would support the world-state against the aggressor group. Under this kind of pressure, and devoid of the military power with which to defy the world-state, the aggressor group will have to give up its aggression.

C. The Pax Islamica in History

The first world-state which envisaged humanity as its citizenry, which was given the first written constitution in history, and which was based upon a divine law unchangeable by the whim of politicians, humans, leaders or by majorities of the ruled, and where ultimately God was the Basis and Guarantor, was founded in Madinah in 622. Upon its coming into being, Muslims and Jews were its constituents. Later, Christians, Zoroastrians, Hindus and Buddhists were added on equal par. It included almost all the ethnicities of the world, at least in part and produced one of the greatest civilizations of all times to which everybody contributed and in which everybody participated — Jews, Christians, Zoroastrians, Hindus and Buddhists by the millions. Under the Rashidun Caliphs, the Umawīs and 'Abbāsīs, it was for the most part an integral world-mass. It was divided and very wide segments of it reconsolidated under the Mughals, the Ayyūbīs, the Fāṭimīs, etc., and finally under the 'Uthmānīs (Ottomans).

Without a doubt, the Islamic universal state had seen up's and down's in its long history. It has known great and small caliphs, great and small sultans and administrators. It was and remained great despite them all. Indeed, the political turbulence noticeable in the violent succession of regimes was superficial and insignificant, precisely, because underneath all the storms was the solid homogeneity of the faith. The lives of the most ethnically diverse Muslim peoples were governed by one and the same *shari'ah*, the law of Islām. Whereas non-Muslim communities governed their own lives by their own non-Muslim laws, all citizens knew their rights and dutires under the *shari'ah* and pursued them with success. For Islāmic justice was available to anyone free of fees or charges. It was available at the local court; for every court in Islām has jurisdiction over all matters, including those affecting the highest executive office, the persons of the caliph and his viziers and the constitution of the state. Moreover, Islāmic justice was available even to the non-citizen, whether Muslim or non-Muslim. For the *shari'ah* recognizes as legal persons endowed with full rights under the law, both the corporate bodies as well as the individuals, the citizens as well as the non-citizens.

Even the advent of colonialism and its tyrannical impositions upon the Muslim World did not succeed in breaking up this unity. Each Western colonial power introduced its own criminal, civil, procedural, commercial and administrative laws into that part of the Muslim World it colonized. The personal status laws, however, remained to this day and everywhere the exclusive domain of the *shari'ah*. Nor could colonialism alter the dominion of the *shari'ah* in non-Muslim affairs. Christian and Jewish courts continued to operate as before under British and French colonialism; and Christian and Islāmic courts continue to operate under Israeli occupation.

The *shari'ah* was responsible for the public order and security the countless millions of humans have enjoyed under its aegis, from Dakar to Mindanao, Samarkand to Dār al Salām, during the centuries-long political dominion of Islām. The change of leadership at the top or of the political regime in the distant capital did not affect the order of daily life which continued to be governed by the *shari'ah*. The *shari'ah* prevented the various segments of the world-*ummah* from aggressing upon one another, the would-be aggressors being fully certain that the whole weight of the *ummah* would fall upon them if they carried out their evil plans. And when aggression did take place, it was the authority of the *shari'ah* that solved the dispute, restored order and peace, and obliged the aggressor to withdraw and undo the damage.

Likewise, the *shari'ah* was responsible for safeguarding the peace between the Islāmic state and any other state, corporate body or alien individual with whom the Islāmic state entered into a covenant of peace. Were it not for the *shari'ah* whose authority and source are divine, the change of political regime or of the mood or whimsy of the ruler might have revoked, denied or unilaterally rescinded any agreement or coventant made. Concluded under the *shari'ah*, every covenant became a covenant whose witness and guard is God. That is why at the height of its power, the Islāmic world-state honored its commitment to abide by any agreement made with the least state or individual.

91

Finally, compared with the United Nations, the *Pax Islamica* is a far more efficient form of social organization. The *Pax Islamica* is based on immutable divine laws. Hence, entry into, exit from, and dealing with it ocult not be the object of *ad hoc* negotiation. The law of the *shari'ah* is one and the same; its jurisdiction, sources and applications are public, known to all, as well as immutable. The *shari'ah* has no countenance for any two states colluding for evil and aggression; nor for any *ummah* to use the right of veto to undo the agreement and cooperation of others to do the good. Backed by the Islāmic state which is its servant, it has the coercive power to restrain or push back any aggression by the strong upon the weak. In every respect, the *Pax Islamica* is better than the United Nations. It is ethical, just and effective in bringing the strong and the weak to follow the straight path of God.

NOTES

1. *Bulletin of the Atomic Scientists*, Vol. 35, No. 8, October, 1979.
2. "The Political Dimensions of Theology," *The Journal of Religion*, Vol. 59, No. 2, April, 1979.

GENERAL INDEX

A

'Abbāsī caliphate, 57, 90
Abraham, 9, 13, 14, 21, 27
  faith of, 1-4, 7, 10
  god of, 5, 18
  people of, 26
Abrahamic faith, 11, 18, 82, 87
abrogation, 5, 12
'Ād, 26
Adam, 26, 30, 57, 84
Afghanistan, 23
Africa, 59, 76
Akkad, 59
Alexander, 34
amānah, 61
America, 23
Ancient covenant, 6
Aquinas, St. Thomas, 3, 39, 43,
  44, 45, 47, 48
Arab proverb, 10
Arabia, 57
Arabic language, 3
Arabic lexicography, 12, 54
Aristotle, 39
'Aṣabīyah, 57
Asia, 59, 76
Augustine, 39, 40, 41, 43,
  45, 46, 47, 48
Aushwitz, 68
Ayatollah, Khomeini, 66, 68
Ayyūbī rulers, 90

B

Babel, 35
Babylon, 41, 42, 59
baptism, 14
Barry, Niaky, 11
Bahya ibn Paquda, 3
Bea, Cardinal, 5
Beer-Sheva, 18
Begin, Menahim, 29, 67
Berlin, 88
Bible, 1, 2, 4, 15, 16, 20, 21, 64
biblical scholars, 28
books, sacred, 2, 4
Brotherhood Movement, the, 63
Broumana Colloquium, 10
Buber, Martin, 8, 10, 33, 36
Buddhists, 60, 90
Burma, 24

C

Caesar, 2, 40
Calvin, John, 39
Camp David Accords, 31
Camus, Albert, 48
Capitoline gods, 2
Carter, Jimmy, 31
Catholic Church, the, 5, 6, 58, 59,
  71, 72, 73, 78, 79, 80
Catholic community, 79
Catholic thought, 39
Catholicism, 73
Chicago, 88

Christ, 4, 6, 39, 72
Christian,
  belief, 4
  community, 71, 79
  doctrine, 5
  dogma, 61
  history, 19
  soteriology, 61
  thought, 42, 78
  West, the, 22, 44
Christianity, 2, 5, 7, 8, 9, 13, 15,
  16, 17, 20, 23, 27, 28, 36,
  51, 57, 61, 62, 81, 85, 87
Christians, 19, 23, 25, 26, 27, 28,
  60, 85, 90
Church, the, 12, 58, 80, 86
Colombia, 77
Colonialism, 54, 82, 86, 88, 91
conscientious objection, 73, 74, 75
Constantinople, 3
constitution, 60, 72, 78, 86, 90
Cordoba, 3
covenant, 6, 32, 35, 37, 57, 91
crusade, 3

D

da'wah, 9
Dakar, 91
Dar al Salam, 91
Declaration of Religious Freedom,
  5, 10
deicide, 16
Deir Yāsīn, 23
dialogue, 2, 4, 10, 20, 21
diaspora, 64
dīn al fiṭrah, 26
divination, 27
doctrine, 5

E

Eckhart, Meister, 1
encounter, 2, 4
encyclical, 73, 78
Eritrea, 24
Ethiopia, 24
evangelical "free" churches, 71
Eve, 84
evil, 26, 33, 36, 38, 53, 55,
  75, 76, 77, 89, 92
exegesis, 5, 12
Europe, 59, 83
exile, 36, 65

F

faith, 2-6, 11, 14, 18, 26, 28, 66,
  68, 69, 78, 79, 84, 86, 90
Fārūqī, Prof. al, 67, 68, 88
fasting, 6
Fāṭimī rulers, 90
Fichte, 59
Fiṭrah, 25, 26

G

Genesis, 35, 43
genocide, 23, 24
Gilkey, Langdon, 83
Gospel
  of Christ, 10
  message, 74
Gospels, 5
Gremillion, Msgr. Joseph, 68
Gush, Emunim, 66

H

Halevy, Judah, 7

Hammurabi, 27, 59
Hannibal, 40
Harkabi, Yehoshafat, 67
Harvard Seminar, 63, 67, 68
Hasdai ibn Shaprut, 84
Hausa, 54
Havana, 68
Hayyūy ibn Zakariīyā, 84
Hebrew
    Bible, 15, 16
    language, 3, 13
    prophets, 31
Hehir, J. Bryan, 71, 72
henotheism, 41
hermeneutics, 15
Hindus, 60, 90
history, 1, 2, 20, 26, 27, 36, 41,
    43, 51, 52, 56, 78, 83, 84
    Christian, 39
    development, 21
    European, 58
Hobbes, John, 41
Holy See, 71, 72
human rights, 24, 72, 77, 78, 79,
    82, 86

I

Ibn Rushd, 3
ideology, 68, 83
Idi Amin, 66
idolatry, 15, 66, 86
idols, 7
'Imrān, 27
India, 24
inspiration, 1
Interreligious Peace Colloquium
Iran, 23, 24, 66, 67
Irenaeus, 43

Isaac, Jules, 5
Isaac, the prophet (Isḥāq), 13, 14,
    28
Islām, 3, 5, 7, 13, 15, 16, 17, 19,
    20, 21, 24-29, 38, 49, 53, 54,
    55, 56, 57, 60, 61, 63, 64, 67,
    81, 82, 84, 85, 86, 87, 89, 91
Islāmic rennaisance, 66
Ismāʻīl, 28
Israel, 2, 4, 11, 13, 14, 17, 18, 22,
    34, 63, 64, 65, 66, 67, 91

J

Jacob, (Yaʻqūb), 13, 14, 28, 86
Jahm ibn Ṣafwān, 85
Jerusalem, 42
Jesus, 8, 9, 15, 17, 28, 29, 44, 59
Jewish
    faith, 8
    identity, 66
    peoplehood, 63
    sacred history, 16
    scriptures, 20
John of Paris, 39
Jonah, 4
Judaic tradition, 31
Judaism, 5, 7, 9, 13, 14, 16, 17,
    18, 19, 20, 24, 28, 29, 38, 63,
    64, 66, 83, 87, 89
Judeo-Christian tradition, 24
judgement, 6
justice, 6, 37, 44, 45, 47, 50, 63,
    64, 67, 68, 73, 78, 82, 83, 84,
    91

K

Kaddafi, 66

95

16, 17
North Africa, 41

O

Old Testament, 6, 20, 86
original sin, 61
Ottomans, 91

P

pacifism, 73, 75
paganism, 2
Pakistan, 66, 68
Palestinians, 22, 82, 84, 88
papacy, 74
paradise, 7
Paul, the apostle, 20, 21
Pax Islamica, 89, 90, 92
peace, 6, 7, 32, 40, 63, 65-68,
    72, 73, 77, 78, 79, 82,
    83, 84, 89, 91
Pedersen, J., 32
pereat mundis, 88
persecution, 5
Persian language, 54
Philippines, 23
Philistines, 33
Pope, the, 5, 22, 44, 45
Pope,
    John XXIII, 5, 73, 74, 77, 78,
    79
    John Paul II, 5, 78, 79
    Paul VI, 52, 73, 76, 77, 78
    Pious XII, 73, 75
polytheism, 25, 41
prayer, 6, 9
prophecy, 26, 27
prophets, 2, 6, 21, 26, 27, 28, 29,

33, 34, 64, 65, 84
Protestant Church, 71
Protocols of the Elders of Zion, 67

Q

qawmīyah, 57, 58
Qur'ān, 8, 12, 26, 27, 28, 29, 53,
    54, 55

R

racism, 55
Rashidūn Caliphate, 90
reason, 25, 39, 40, 41, 43, 44, 47
Reformation, the, 58
religio naturalis, 25, 26, 85
religion, 10, 11, 15, 16, 19, 20, 21,
    24, 25, 26, 27, 28, 29 33,
    36, 37, 41, 46, 47, 48, 54,
    58, 59, 60, 61, 65, 68, 69,
    82, 83, 84, 86
revelation, 27, 28, 29, 38, 39, 87
Roman Empire, 40, 81
Romans, 2
romanticism, 59
Rome, 41, 44
Roy, Cardinal Maurice, 74

S

Saadia, Gaon Fayyūmīyā, 84
sabbath, 21
Sabians, 4, 28
sacraments, 86
Sadat, Anwar, 31
saints, 34, 41
Samarkand, 91
Samuel, the Prophet, 33

Samuel ibn Nagdala, 84
Sanhedrin, 29
Santayana, George, 32
Sargon of Akkad, 27
Saudi Arabia, 67
Sawahili, 54
Schechemites, 86
Schleiermacher, 59
science, 27, 37, 81
scripture, 20, 28, 29, 87
self, the, 41
Shah of Iran, 66
Sharī'ah, 54, 60, 84, 90, 91, 92
Shirk, 25
Shu'ūbīyah, 57
sin, 1, 33, 39
Smith, Wilfred Cantwell, 65, 69
Somalia, 24
soul, 32, 34, 41
St. Thomas Aquinas, 3, 39, 43,
    44, 45, 47, 48
synagogue, 12
Synod of Bishops, 74
Syria, 59, 68

T

Talmudic Rabbis, 31
Taqlīd, 52
Tawḥīd, 84
Taylor, John, 7, 8
Tehran, 23
Temple, William, 8
Thailand, 24
Thamūd, 27
Theology, 18, 33, 77, 84
Third World, 59, 68
Tigris-Euphrates Valley, 59
Toledo, 3

Torah, 13-17, 20, 29, 64,
    65, 66, 67, 83
traditions, 2, 39, 52, 53
    religious, 24, 27, 36
    semitic, 26
trinity, the, 4, 15, 16, 29
Turkish language, 54

U

Uganda, 66
'Umar ibn al Khaṭṭāb, 87
Ummah, 8, 55, 57, 58, 60, 61,
    63, 67, 83, 91, 92
Umawīs, 90
United Nations, 22, 24, 35, 61
United States, 10, 22, 46
Universal Declaration of Human
    Rights, 79
Urdu, 54
Uri Simon, 66
'Uthmānīi rulers, 90
Utopianism, 35, 36

V

Vallier, Ivan, 71, 72
values, 1, 6, 7, 8, 19, 43, 53,
    56, 63, 86, 88
Vatican, 10, 29, 72
Vatican Council, the Second, 5,
    10, 63, 72, 73, 75, 78
Vietnam, 74

W

West Bank, the 67
Wolof proverb, 10

World Council of Churches, 10, 29, 46
worship, 25, 67

Y

Ya'qūb, see Jacob

Z

Zionism, 68
Zionists, 23
Zoroastrians, 60, 90

INDEX OF QUR'ÀNIC VERSES

INDEX OF BIBLICAL VERSES